.

PRAISE FOR *LISTEN IN*

"The issues related to race in the workplace that are presented by the characters are too often experienced today. *Listen In* empowers its readers to be change agents with simple, yet concrete steps for self-improvement and for developing systemic change in the workplace. This book is a phenomenal resource and exceptional value for an individual and organization to invest in. It is a must-read and applicable not only to corporate settings but also to institutions of higher education and beyond."

—DR. ANIKA BISSAHOYO, Bowie State University

"*Listen In* is the source for addressing race in the workplace today. The conversations are real and relevant and provide thought-provoking insights to anyone who is curious and courageous enough to read them. Allison has bridged the gap between 'corporate speak' and actually dealing with the everyday issues that exist for minorities in the workplace."

—CYNTHIA GOINS, principal of Motivations

"*Listen In* is the groundbreaking new resource for understanding workplace diversity. This book brings a fresh lens to addressing topics of race and diversity. Readers will be entertained and feel empowered and inspired to have tough conversations that will greatly impact workplace relations."

—DR. COURTNEY R. CORNICK, psychologist

"What a read! I love what Allison has done to present a conversation that most companies are reluctant to engage in. *Listen In* should be required reading for all C-suite leaders and HR professionals. Corporations that are not leveraging all of their talent should not be mistaken as a viable business in the twenty-first century. Thank you for sharing a tough conversation."

—JANE C. SMITH, president and chief results
officer of Next Level Consulting

"*Listen In* will be catalytic in changing corporate environments to value diversity. This book combines the real-life conversations that people of color are having and the prevailing white privilege that stagnates their career growth with real-life solutions. Allison Manswell brilliantly weaves the stories and solutions with the expertise of a master coach, experience of a senior HR professional, and the compassion of someone who cares deeply about moving our country forward."

—REV. WILLIAM T. CHANEY JR., new church
strategist, United Methodist Church

LISTEN IN

LISTEN IN

CRUCIAL CONVERSATIONS ON
RACE IN THE WORKPLACE

ALLISON MANSWELL

Advantage | Books

Published by Advantage, Charleston, South Carolina.
Member of Advantage Media.

ADVANTAGE is a registered trademark, and the Advantage colophon is a trademark of Advantage Media Group, Inc.

Printed in the United States of America.

10 9 8 7 6 5 4 3 2 1

ISBN: 978-1-64225-969-8 (Hardcover)
ISBN: 978-1-64225-968-1 (eBook)

Library of Congress Control Number: 2024905424

Cover and layout design by Lance Buckley.

This publication is designed to provide accurate and authoritative information in regard to the subject matter covered. It is sold with the understanding that the publisher is not engaged in rendering legal, accounting, or other professional services. If legal advice or other expert assistance is required, the services of a competent professional person should be sought.

To my sons, family members, and friends,
thank you for the love that gives me the courage to speak my peace.

To Eli, Shane, LaToya, Roshunda, and Maya,
thank you for choosing me.

To my mother, my father, and all the ancestors
whose sacrifice made this experience possible—thank you.

CONTENTS

INTRODUCTION

This book wrote itself. About six months after Sheryl Sandberg released the book *Lean In: Women, Work, and the Will to Lead*, I was chatting with a friend, and I asked her, "When is someone going to write a book about being Black at work?"

She said, "When you do it."

Even though I immediately brushed off the idea, the suggestion continued to bounce around in my head. It wouldn't leave me alone. The concept, format, and dialogue continued to talk to me, often distracting me so much that I had to write it down.

Meanwhile, 2015 brought the summer of my discontent; an unsettling barrage of police brutality incidents, the South Carolina church massacre, and hashtag overload. The notes for this book became the place where I could process my emotions, debate the issues, and design business solutions that could make a difference.

Toni Morrison says, "If there is a book you really want to read but it hasn't been written yet, then you must write it." She didn't mention the inherent risks of making that book available to the public. I had to get comfortable with the potential criticism and strong opinions of others. Once I did that, I took the leap and began writing this work of fiction, self-help, and business consulting.

And now nine years after *Listen In* was originally published, I am re-releasing it with the sequel. None of the content was changed and unfortunately, it feels just as relevant. The combination of both books in this series has the potential to create a new ending.

"When we deny our stories, they define us.
When we own our stories, we get to write the ending."
—BRENÉ BROWN

So why take such a narrow focus on the African American perspective?

1. The foundation of the business case for diversity and inclusion hinges on the premise that everyone's point of view and contribution is essential to the bottom line. Race is a factor in every aspect of American life and culture. However, I find that the African American point of view is absent from boardrooms and watercoolers, diminishing the collaboration and innovation that has the potential to naturally flourish when people understand and trust each other.

2. The foundation of the obstacles we see in African American communities are economic challenges caused by generations of disparities in having access to quality education and jobs. For most families, their economy is funded by the employment income that is accessible to them. So by addressing the issues around race in the workplace, over time we can close the gap on these disparities and move closer to solving broader community challenges.

3. The core of our humanity is said to hinge on our care and concern for each other as human beings. To me, the jury is out on whether Black lives really matter on Main Street. So maybe (just maybe) if we help Wall Street take the lead and help them realize that #blackmoneymatters and #blacktalentmatters, the case for Black lives becomes unnecessary.

I realize that conversations about race at work are awkward and difficult. It seems to me that the awkwardness and difficulty come from the absence of a safe context to host the interaction and lack of awareness to guide productive dialogue. My intention is for this book to provide that context of mutual understanding, nonjudgment, and genuine desire to build stronger relationships. My goal is to help individuals develop the skills to have these conversations, plan their careers effectively, and transform organizations to solve problems that live behind the metrics.

A few important disclaimers:

1. I don't pretend to represent all African Americans (US-born people of African descent) or Black people (foreigners of African descent who live in the US) with the views expressed in this book.

2. Not every company has the organizational culture or metrics expressed in this book.

3. This is a novel with fictional characters and situations. The characters and situations are a figment of my imagination. Any similarities to individuals (living or dead) are purely coincidental and simply provide proof that these experiences are valid. In part 2, the resources are based on the subject matter expertise that I have gained from my education and twenty-five-plus years of experience working in talent management, learning and leadership development, and organizational effectiveness. They are not based on any particular company, organization, or agency.

4. Not everyone should engage in conversations about race at work. There are people who lack the personal and social awareness, communication and relationship skills, emotional maturity, and range of experience to be a productive part of this sensitive conversation. This book isn't for them. If you engage in conversation with someone who fits this description, I urge you to remember this paragraph and politely excuse yourself.

LISTEN IN

A. allows us to eavesdrop on a series of candid conversations that give us insight into various perspectives on societal challenges, our workplace, and their impact on individuals and teams; and

B. gives personal and organizational development resources to transform our lives and our companies.

I could have spent inordinate amounts of time and energy to include research and statistics; however, I don't think we lack data. We already have all the information we need. Every time someone reads this book and nods, relates the characters to their experience or that of a friend or family member—that is powerful validation. I chose the format of a story with lots of dialogue as a deliberate strategy to

A. promote active listening: observing a fishbowl conversation forces you to tune in to what the characters are experiencing while (hopefully) putting your internal chatter on pause.

B. offer raw emotion: operating in a sterile corporate world where we focus on products and process often causes us to forget that the human resources department is actually run by real people. They have hopes and dreams like everyone else, and at the end of the day they are trying to make a better life for their families.

C. change the conversation: engaging in meaningful dialogue is the only path to solving some of the workplace challenges that slow productivity, contribute to employee disengagement, and ultimately hamper innovation.

D. emphasize that research is not the answer: we need people in positions of power or with related influence to make decisions that change the outcomes. That's it. That's all. We can stop hiding behind studies and metrics—just do things differently.

Now that I have outlined my intentions, let me admit the discomfort that this book brings.

"Walking into our stories of hurt can feel dangerous. But the process of regaining our footing in the midst of struggle is where our courage is tested, and our values are forged. Our stories of struggle can be big ones, like the loss of a job or the end of a relationship, or smaller ones, like a conflict with a friend or colleague. Regardless of magnitude or circumstance, the rising strong process is the same: We reckon with our emotions and get curious about what we're feeling; we rumble with our stories until we get to a place of truth; and we live this process, every day, until it becomes a practice and creates nothing short of a revolution in our lives. Rising strong after a fall is how we cultivate wholeheartedness."
—BRENÉ BROWN, *RISING STRONG*

THE RECKONING. THE RUMBLE. THE REVOLUTION.

This book includes all three elements: the pain of reckoning, the conflict of rumble, and the risk of revolution. The discomfort is not my deliberate intention, but I'm okay with it as an outcome. I am inspired by people like Stuart Scott, who led ESPN through its initial discomfort with him to the impact he is credited for today. This book will immerse you in the characters' journey to personal and professional fulfillment. More than any other outcome, my hope is that it inspires you to embark on a journey of your own.

PART I

❶
REFINED BY FIRE

Shane swaggered through the restaurant door; his six-foot-three frame and "win you over" smile moved through the crowded space with a confidence only he could pull off. It was hard not to notice him. The air-conditioning immediately went to work and dried the sweat droplets that had formed on his forehead from the sweltering DC weather. He scanned the room until he saw his friend Elijah waving him over to a large round table filled with familiar faces.

"Late again." Elijah laughed as Shane slid into a seat.

"Hey, man, don't give me a hard time. You know I'm trying to make VP. Doesn't matter what time you start. It only matters what time you leave." Shane, a former marine, had been the director of supply chain for eight years. He was known for having the unique and complimentary qualities of being a strategic and engaging leader. His peers raved about his ability to balance efficient operations with exceptional people skills, and although he had a reputation for being tough, every interaction left those around him feeling heard and clear on next steps. He was very successful at balancing strong leadership and personability. Those who knew him were well aware of the storm that lay just beneath that warm, fluffy cloud.

"You'll get there soon, Shane." Maya's soft-spoken voice was hard to hear over the buzz of the restaurant. Her warm and nurturing demeanor always made everyone feel better. At fifty-seven, she was the oldest of the group, but unlike some of the others, she hadn't gone as far in the business world. She was reserved and not always willing to talk for the sake of being heard. She listened intently and often only shared her opinions after much introspection and a degree of certainty about her information. Coworkers and leaders often assumed she didn't have a point of view or maybe that she didn't process information as quickly as the extroverts in her circle. She had no problem being in the background and often let others take credit for her ideas. Maya wanted to pursue higher rungs on the corporate ladder but made a conscious decision not to change core elements of herself to fit in. So she put her emotional energy into nurturing her family and building a thriving small business. It was comforting to know that she could retire at any moment a menopause symptom told her she should.

"Oh, honey, please! Be careful what you wish for! As soon as I made director, it was like people expected me to be on call twenty-four hours a day. There is no such thing as time off anymore," LaToya chimed in. When LaToya spoke, people listened. It was clear to anyone who met her why she was so well respected in her company. Her confidence came across in everything she did and was sometimes mistaken for arrogance. But those who took the time to engage in real conversation with her quickly discovered that she was one of the most emotionally intelligent leaders in her company. She simply processed information, interpreted meaning, and articulated her perspective at the speed of light. She was very open to other ideas, quick to extract lessons learned, and very effective at foreseeing outcomes quickly. But one area she clearly needed to work on was leaving room for others to participate in the process. Her career trajectory reflected her reputation as a "get it done, grace under fire, and take no prisoners" leader.

However, she often wondered how much of her life she had sacrificed at the altar of her career.

Roshunda sat to Maya's left and was the last member of the group to speak. She had a sweet voice and sassy energy. At twenty-five years old, Roshunda was the youngest of the group and was proud of her millennial status. She had an impressive combination of Ivy League education and Fortune 10 experience. She also had a powerfully seductive energy. Every male in the bar glanced her way at one point or another. And because she was so accustomed to the attention, she was able to be polite and dismissive in the same gesture.

"That's an old-school mentality, to 'live to work.' Business acumen begins at home for me. I didn't sell my employer twenty-four-hour access to me. When there is a key deliverable—I'm all over it. I will work long and hard around the clock until it's done. But during normal operations, I don't answer WOA emails after 8:00 p.m. I use my downtime for activities that rest my brain and empower me. Shame on you if you don't learn to put boundaries on your time."

Elijah chimed in. "I must be getting old, but what is a WOA email? Did your generation make up a new acronym that's about to get into the dictionary?"

"No, that one is all mine. It means 'whirlwind of activity': a question or action where responding off hours won't add value or contribute to the bottom line. Therefore, it can wait until the next business day. You also need to read Ariana Huffington's book *Thrive*. Our nation needs a new definition of success that includes our well-being. I don't need a broken cheekbone to figure that out."

Meeting for comfort food and conversation was their mental health ritual. LaToya, Roshunda, Maya, Shane, and Elijah had been wonderful friends who had become family over twelve years. Despite having families and busy corporate and community service schedules, they made time to connect on a regular basis to share their successes and struggles.

Elijah raised his glass and announced, "It always feels so good to get together with my peeps and decompress. Let my hair down, if you will."

"Get outta here with your bald head. What do you know about letting your hair down?" joked LaToya.

"I know it's unbe-weave-able how long your hair got since the last time I saw you," Elijah replied with a big smile.

"You know a sista gotta do what a sista gotta do. Until corporate America learns to accept me in all my nappy glory, it's gonna be me and this weave all the way." She was unapologetically blunt.

Shane winked at LaToya as Roshunda rolled her eyes in disapproval. LaToya continued, "I'm taking the Hillary Clinton approach. I ain't lettin' some relaxer steal my dreams of being CEO. I will play the game until I slay the game."

"I hear you, but what the hell does that have to do with Hillary Clinton?" asked Elijah.

"Ah, see, y'all missed it. You remember the whole Monica Lewinsky scandal? I kept trying to figure out why Hillary wasn't moved by that. I kept watching every day to see when she was going to snap and go ballistic on Bill. But she never did, did she? It took me until the first round of Democratic candidate debates in 2008 to figure out what she was thinking. 'What in the world does a blow job have to do with me being president?' Sista Girl didn't let that distraction deter her from her goal. And look, she made sure she pursued that goal—as planned. That's where we can all take a page outta her book. Don't let this hair issue in corporate America take you off the path to your goals. One by one we won't change anything about how people see natural hair or braids. But collectively, when we all get to the C-suite, we can take our weave out in the boardroom if we feel like it. We need to use the fire in our lives to refine us like gold and then step out and shine."

"But wait a minute," Maya chimed in, "if we all take that approach, change never happens. My soul didn't come to this earth to conform. I have no desire to fit in. I left a six-figure position because the stress of being a good fit was just too much for me. If my natural hair was too much of a distraction for them, then they didn't deserve my discretionary effort. I found another company where I was truly valued for what is under my hair."

"You know what?" Roshunda shifted in her seat and leaned in. "I think you guys are overreacting. I just don't think that hair is that big of an issue. I have been successful in all hairstyles: braids, weave, I even did a non-blow-dried, natural Afro-looking style for a minute. All that matters is the results you produce."

Maya's demeanor changed. Her normally quiet and subdued energy swelled into a tsunami wave. "Well, ain't that some shit? Do you have any idea, much less the willingness to acknowledge, the sacrifice your ancestors made so that your narrow behind could sit here years later and say out of your mouth that it doesn't matter? Your generation infuriates me with your 'Racism is over' mentality. You probably have never seen the Black name / white name résumé experiment or the pay disparity data between Blacks and whites. Check up on those results and get back to me about 'It doesn't matter.'"

The room went silent, and it felt like the oxygen had been sucked out of the atmosphere. Everyone who knew Maya had experienced her transition from a mild-mannered, soft-spoken wallflower to a militant soldier who channeled Harriet Tubman's energy.

Eli broke the awkward silence. "All three of you are right," he said. "Roshunda, there are some environments where hair doesn't matter. And those enlightened corporate cultures will corner the market and outperform other companies in the long run. Eventually corporate America will figure out that people have enough to deal with in their normal lives than to be worried about fitting in at work. That emotional energy can be redirected into innovative ideas that will become the next iPad and change their industry."

Elijah continued, "Maya, for some people, picking up and rolling out is not an option, in which case LaToya's point is a good one. First, clarify what kind of culture you're in. Not what's on the posters and in the diversity and inclusion report but what is really valued in your organization. Become situationally aware of the style, flow, and vibe of senior execs. Then, do whatever your checkbook allows you to do. If you can afford to be a change agent—go for it. If you need that job at that moment, get a relaxer, get a keratin treatment, just get something that will get you by Monday to Friday. Then *do you* for real on the weekend. But either way be purposeful about your decision. Stop being emotional about your hair and start being strategic. Have you seen Hanna on Tyler Perry's *The Haves and the Have Nots*? That sister will switch it up as necessary. My bald-headed opinion is that Black women need to take control of this narrative," Elijah interjected. "Get clear about the culture you're working in, and get comfortable with the hair you wear. When you do that, corporate America will follow your lead."

Eli had a way of schooling folks and adding emotional punctuation to a conversation. Somehow it felt like the bell had just rung.

2

JIM LISTENS IN

J im was the CEO of a company with over 18,000 employees. He had the standard pedigree of education and experience and had been groomed for his current role by the previous chairman of the board before he retired. He was proud of his success and prided himself on his diverse background and open-minded parenting. He wasn't sure how he ended up at a table within earshot of this conversation. He wasn't intending to eavesdrop but couldn't help but be intrigued by the Hillary-Clinton-blow-job comment. After that, he was hooked into the conversation. He found himself incredibly curious about how his company was experienced by African American employees. What would they say if they got together in a restaurant? Did hair really matter that much? Did their company culture engage all employees equally? All of a sudden, he had a flurry of questions worth asking his leadership team.

3

MY FAMILY'S INTELLECTUAL PROPERTY

The sunset painted its beauty behind the DC skyline as spring discreetly turned to summer. Unfortunately, LaToya was too distracted to notice. She was running late to meet everyone for drinks and was determined to squeeze the last ounce of value out of the conference before leaving to meet her friends. Her spontaneous and often impulsive personality didn't lend itself well to punctuality. However, she had developed some personal discipline for being on time because of how important it was in the work environment. Personal growth and career development were at the core of her being, so she always made time for worthwhile learning experiences. She valued the time to connect, exchange ideas, and support others personally and professionally. She couldn't wait to share all she had learned with her crew.

As LaToya made her way across the restaurant parking lot, she could smell the tantalizing aroma of Caribbean food and hear the familiar sounds of reggae music. This was a popular happy hour destination where they could enjoy tasty cuisine and island vibes in the background. Her phone rang, and Elijah came up on her caller ID. "Hi, sweetie. I'm almost there. You can actually see me walking in right now," she said as she entered the restaurant.

Elijah and the rest of the group were awaiting her arrival at the VIP table in the back. They all turned around and gave her a big smile. "Hello, sweetheart, I'm so happy you made it," said Elijah with sincerity. "I knew traffic would be a mess, and you must be tired from traveling all day. Thought you might cancel on us."

"Nah, man, we have to make time for the things that are important to us. Don't get me wrong, this conference was important too. But at the end of the day it's our loved ones and friends that enrich our lives. You guys are the big rocks in my jar." LaToya's reference to the age-old time management metaphor was a great reminder of why they kept their Happy Hour Happenings on the books, no matter how much rescheduling had to be done.

"So tell us about the conference," Roshunda said. "This must be about the third one you've been to this year."

"Okay, before I even get started about the conference, let me start with a little context." Everyone knew this would take more than a minute, once LaToya got started on a conversation about learning. Her approach and language were so direct that people often branded her as a know-it-all. The characterization was ironic given the fact that her whole approach to life was centered around the idea that we are all here to learn and grow from lessons of our own and those from others. She was always listening for what she could learn from someone else's life.

"We need a new way of looking at career development. If you sit around thinking that your boss or your company is responsible for your development, you will be waiting a long time for an opportunity that won't arrive. Your career is your responsibility. In fact, it is your family's intellectual property. Just like how every company has IP that generates revenue for the business, the development that goes in your head and translates into tangible application of skills is your family's intellectual property that will generate revenue as a salary. In addition to the conferences and formal trainings that I go to, I also have an advocate and a sponsor at work."

"What is an advocate, and what is a sponsor?" asked Roshunda. "Do you mean a mentor?"

LaToya replied, "No, you see … everyone thinks you need to have a mentor. So they run around asking people to mentor them. Don't get me wrong, mentors are important. Everyone needs an honest sounding board who will tell them the truth. If your mentor is not making you uncomfortable, then you need a new mentor. My experience has been that the best mentoring relationships are spontaneous, natural, and organic. But that's another story. More importantly, what we as African Americans need are advocates within our company. Or better yet, a sponsor who will lend their credibility on your behalf."

Everyone could feel LaToya's passion and knew that she would spend the entire evening on this topic if they let her.

"Okay, so here we go," Roshunda said sarcastically. Every time I get together with you people, something comes up about race. Can we talk about something else?"

Maya jumped into the conversation for the first time. "Sure we can. Let's talk about how only 14 percent of the general male population is over six feet tall and 60 percent of CEOs are over six feet. Would that be a more comfortable conversation, Roshunda?"

Shane interrupted them. "That statistic is only valid for white boys. If you are a brother over five foot seven, you get coaching on how others find you intimidating. No one knows what to do with that bullshit. And it almost sounds like others want you to be present but invisible, like a butler."

LaToya shook her head and continued, "People might not always be willing to admit the realities of unconscious bias in the workplace, but my experience is that most successful executives are willing to vouch for diverse candidates who they know can deliver results. Sometimes they want to be discreet. That's why advocacy and sponsorship are so powerful. An advocate will literally advocate taking a chance on you when you may not be present in the conversation. That person might be willing to tell others about good work that you have done for them. A sponsor goes a step further, and maybe even lends bits and pieces of their credibility and or reputation to endorse you. Needless to say, if you are a person of color or any other diverse candidate, it helps when these people are members of the majority."

"So let me see if I got this right. You mean to tell me that you got white boys, maybe even good ole boys, to advocate on your behalf when you are not in the room?" Maya asked.

"Yup. I sure did," LaToya proudly continued. Maya looked at her, and there were one thousand meaningful words in her millisecond glance. "I know what you're thinking, Maya. And the answer is no, I didn't sell my soul or give up the cookie to get the endorsement either."

"I never said that," Maya replied, trying to sound innocent. "However, the little voice from your coworkers was screaming it in my ears," she continued as she burst out laughing.

"Yes, I know, completely ludicrous, isn't it? That a hardworking, diva-looking, value-adding Black woman could gain a white man's respect without sleeping with him. I know that's what my colleagues are thinking, but I don't give a shit. I know my worth, and I know the value I bring. I refuse to be moved by their small-mindedness that is stuck in a time warp. Sometimes I'm sad that they devalue my contribution to the point of a sex favor. But then I shake it off and realize that white women have the same challenge. And it is really their low self-esteem that shines brighter in the afterglow of my light."

"Preach that!" Shane leaned over and kissed LaToya lovingly near her ear. "They don't know that you save your cookie for me," he announced.

"And you bring the milk," LaToya quipped. Then they looked at each other with an intensity that implied many lifetimes of being lovers. Their individual personalities were like thunder and lightning. But somehow, they were able to maintain a relationship that felt like the calm after a storm.

LaToya got so lost in the moment that she almost forgot what they were talking about. Finally, she snapped back to reality and continued, "They are just flattering themselves to think that they're my type. But if it makes them feel good—whatever. As long as that check cashes every two weeks."

Roshunda jumped in and said, "Okay, great. I'm just tickled that you two soulmates got the cookies-and-milk situation worked out. But can we get back to the key takeaways from the conference? So far you told us about looking at our career development as intellectual property. Then you made the distinction between a mentor and advocate and a sponsor. Then we got clear about how this evening will end with you and Shane. All life-changing stuff, but I want to hear more about the conference."

"Yes, that's the best part," LaToya continued. "The Listen In Roundtable is a new career and professional development conference designed for people of color. I went to a session specifically designed for women. Roshunda, I know you don't want to hear this because racism is over in your world, but it is a powerful way for Black people to get together and talk about the things that are important to us."

"Okay, so when are they gonna create something for brothers?" Shane asked. "It seems like me and the men I know go to all kinds of seminars and do all kinds of extra projects, but it rarely materializes into an advancement opportunity. It feels like companies would prefer to promote a sister over a brother whenever possible. You know how many people have come to me as trainees and then were rotated and promoted around and above me? We joke about it to keep our sanity, but that shit ain't funny." Shane sat back, and everyone felt the impact of his truth. LaToya kissed his forehead, and they all wished they could make it better.

"The Listen In events are for men and women. We should check for upcoming dates in DC. We have to get out there and take advantage of these opportunities. Somewhere in the last ten years, it went out of style to have such specific events where we gather together. All of a sudden we got cute and didn't want to be singled out from our peers. We wanted to stay within the mainstream because we didn't want anyone to think that we needed a special program. Great in theory. Except that we ain't foolin' anybody. I don't know who we thought we were blending in with. Meanwhile, during our little game of hide-and-seek, the LGBTQIA+ community mobilized themselves, focused on a handful of issues, and pushed their agenda forward. Now we look up and, in seventeen relatively short years after they came out of the closet, they have gotten the rights and benefits that they made a priority for their community. And fifty years after the March on Washington, we're still singing, 'We shall overcome someday.' Can somebody pick a fucking day so we can put it on our calendars?"

Everyone needed a minute to take that in. As offensive as it was to hear, deep in their hearts they believed LaToya was right.

4

SILENCE IS A STATEMENT

STATEMENT №1

"Ain't that some shit." LaToya put down her drink and rolled her eyes in disbelief. She couldn't believe what she was seeing on TV. Baltimore was burning. Familiar buildings up in flames. City officials scrambling for solutions. Breaking news coverage twenty-four seven. "I knew it was only a matter of time before they took a member of the wrong family or started some shit in the wrong city. Well, Baltimore ain't having it. I wonder if they are going to cover the Justice or Else March like they are covering this." LaToya took a sip of her drink and turned around.

Maya chimed in. "Do you hear yourself? That Old Testament thinking of an eye for an eye leaves everyone blind. What those thugs are doing is wrong. Burning down their own city is just stupid."

The two women were clearly on opposite sides of the issue, and this was most certainly not the time for them to engage each other in any kind of "healthy debate." Eli stepped in and said, "Can we just agree that our community is divided on what the right response is? But what we agree on is the fact that a young man died in custody and what we know so far is disturbing."

"Yes, and we also know that all cops aren't bad," Maya blurted out.

"Okay, let's double-click on that for a minute, because I keep hearing that being thrown around. I agree that 100 percent of cops aren't bad; however, 100 percent of the cops in this case either allowed Freddie Gray to bounce around in that police wagon and/or refused to get him the medical assistance he needed. And 0 percent of them tried to stop what was obviously mistreatment of a suspect. Statistically, at least one of the six should have spoken up and this situation would have been avoided. Right, Maya? That's my point. Their silence is a statement that makes them guilty."

When Maya didn't answer, LaToya continued, "Here's the cold, hard truth. Culture is stronger than individuals. So if you have a police code that creates and promotes 'blue code' behavior, then your argument is no longer valid. In this case, 100 percent of the cops were bad. And then when the shit gets to be just too much and powerlessness turns to rioting, everyone is quick to say that riots don't solve anything. You need to go back and look at some of the changes that came as a direct result of the riots in LA after the Rodney King verdict. Bless his soul, that man never recovered. He was one of the first to take his beating in public on video and still didn't get a conviction."

Despite Eli's attempt at mediation, Maya couldn't resist making another point. "And good cops don't get any credit. We just say, 'They were doing their job.' And when a police officer is killed in the line of duty, there are no marches, no media."

LaToya took a deep breath and tried to appear sympathetic. "Sista girl, here's a few ways to understand the difference. First, when a cop is killed, they throw the book at the perpetrator. They put him under the jail and send a clear message of consequences and repercussions. But when a cop or neighborhood watch idiot kills one of us, they get off. Secondly, it's the frequency, too, Maya. Come on. When we start having five to eight of these cases appear on social media and then in the news in the same month—one every twenty-eight hours, to be exact—sane, level-headed human beings are expected to recognize the disparate impact on one segment of the population. Don't insult my intelligence by trying to dismiss the sheer frequency and severity of these cases. Don't pretend you don't see the statistical—if not common sense—evidence that this is wrong."

Maya seemed worn out. Eli jumped in. "Okay, since we're being real. What about Black-on-Black crime?"

"What about it?" LaToya answered as if she had no idea what Eli was talking about.

"I'm so tired of hearing Black and white people talk about Black-on-Black crime whenever there is a case of police brutality. It starts to sound as if, 'Since they kill each other, what's the difference if a cop kills them?' It's offensive. But besides the emotion, let's apply two factors of logic and see if this response still makes sense. Number one: If a white male banker gets killed, we call it a tragedy, don't we? No one says, 'Yeah, well, you know those guys are the ones responsible for the banking debacle of 2008 or 99 percent of white-collar crime in corporations.' Somehow, when it's us, people bring up Black-on-Black crime as if it neutralizes or minimizes the impact of police brutality. It doesn't. They are two different things that don't belong in the same sentence. We are allowed to have more than one serious issue going on in our community at any given time.

"Number two: Let's not pretend that the lack of jobs and opportunity in the inner city is a random coincidence. So when drug dealing is the only viable option to earn—drugs and gun violence are bound to happen. I am not condoning what is happening—we need to do better. But let's also talk about how the drugs got there. Do you think any of those drug dealers have passports? Let's be passionate about getting high-speed internet in the inner city before we start pretending that the violence sprung up on its own. The generation that is coming of age right now is going to challenge our notion of civil rights. Their smartphones don't lie, and they are fed up. The best thing we can do is teach them how to use their energy to make a difference and/ or channel their anger outside of their own community and into something positive. You are welcome to whatever opinion gives you a good night's rest. As for me, I'm willing to call this shit out because I can't imagine losing a child like this. Be careful what you feel strongly about. Life has a way of making a hypocrite out of us."

STATEMENT №2

In the weeks after the unrest in Baltimore, LaToya was still wrestling with the emotional and psychological effects of ongoing killings and other cases of police brutality that came to light after Freddie Gray. She felt sick overhearing coworkers' comments that seemed to demonstrate their complete disregard for Black lives. She refused to engage anyone in conversation without a common ground of understanding. She simply didn't trust her ability to hold her tongue or hold back her tears. She thought to herself, 'I will sit here and burst into flames before I let these motherfuckers see me cry.'

It was a hot summer day, and she was headed out to lunch with Susan Patterson, the VP of HR. After they exchanged greetings and small talk, Susan began. "Thank you for making time for this lunch."

"No problem. I was anxious to hear what's on your mind," LaToya said with a smile.

"Well, you know we have a strong commitment to diversity and inclusion."

Before she could finish, LaToya replied, "I see what we post on the website and posters."

Immediately Susan realized that everything she had heard about LaToya was true—she was a no-bullshit straight shooter. "And that's exactly why we need your help. We would like you to lead a task force to help us understand how we can move the needle on our D&I goals. We want to know how we can recruit more women and people of color. And how we can increase our numbers in senior leadership. We will assemble a multidisciplinary team that will study our current approach, our results to date, internal and external drivers and metrics. The deliverable is a report on what's working, what isn't, and recommendations on solutions." Susan paused and waited for LaToya to interject.

"So what exactly do you need from me?" LaToya questioned.

"Your role will be to lead the team, help them develop an approach to data collection, interpretation, and report out. You would secure the subject matter experts required and confirm any other resources you need. It will be a high-profile assignment that could be very beneficial for your career."

Time seemed to stand still like a scene from *The Matrix*. LaToya had originally been suspicious about this invitation but had accepted out of curiosity. She'd tried to be optimistic, but this moment was confirmation of her worst fear—another invitation to a special assignment. Over the years she'd noted that diverse employees were offered an increasing number of these "opportunities" in which they were required to add more work to their plate and demonstrate that they could accomplish more with less. These assignments were presented as career opportunities that rarely materialized into promotions. While she and the others who had voiced this opinion appreciated the visibility that this offered, the impact was minimized by the fact that white men and white women were often given these roles before they were ready. This allowed them to struggle through them, gain the "learning," and then have their impact overestimated as they were promoted—sometimes way too early. This was the phenomenon that Mama used to call "having to be twice as good to be considered half as qualified." Somehow, today felt like the day that she would politely decline to participate in any more navel-gazing about diversity that failed to address the real issues everyone was hiding from.

"And do you have any other candidates in mind?" LaToya asked, her face free of expression.

"Um … no. Your name came up in every conversation, so I didn't really think of anyone else. I guess I just assumed that, given the level of visibility, you would be interested." Susan was getting nervous that this wasn't going well.

LaToya shifted and got comfortable. She felt her higher self speak to her, and she made a conscious decision that this was an authentic leadership moment for her. She was about to be honest and drop some knowledge that she knew could be career limiting. But it was a chance her soul was begging her to take.

"Susan, thank you so much for thinking of me. But I'm going to decline." LaToya waited for the official invitation to explain what seemed like a hasty decision.

"Okay. But can I ask why you are so certain that you don't want to do this? Would you like some time to think about it?" Susan asked.

"Ironically, I have had a lot of time to think about this. In fact, I have been immersed in our company's D&I approach since I started working here. I have lots of opportunities to observe and then report out when me and my colleagues meet for drinks and talk about our respective companies. And the last few weeks since the rioting in Baltimore, I have been patiently waiting to see evidence of 'our commitment to D&I.' So, I would be happy to explain why I respectfully decline this opportunity. Your approach to recruit me for this is actually an example of why our diversity numbers are embarrassing as you look up the leadership ranks. You identified one candidate that a small group of people endorsed. You decided amongst yourselves that I was a 'good fit' and didn't consider any other options. That happens a lot here, except it's usually white males and a few white females getting the prime visibility assignments. Being an African American woman may have been an advantage in this case, but it isn't usually.

"Terry Simmons developed a concept called *vectors* that helps us understand how different people experience tailwinds and headwinds in organizations. These winds either propel them forward or act as a hindrance to their progress. In this case, being an outspoken African American woman may have worked in my favor to help me be seen as a candidate for the dirty work on this assignment. But in most cases, it wouldn't work that way." LaToya shifted in her seat. "Can I ask a question? Does this company have a position or opinion on police brutality?"

Susan said, "We actually just had this conversation with the executive team. The African American employee group asked us to make a statement after the Freddie Gray thing, and we decided not to get involved in issues like that. If we start that precedent we would have to comment on every other cause, and that just isn't good business strategy based on the broad base of stakeholders we have."

LaToya took a deep breath and softly replied, "That 'Freddie Gray thing' that you just referenced is actually a pretty big life-or-death issue to those who feel at risk of police brutality. By the way, that's 28 percent of our employee base. And although they are predominantly at the bottom of our ranks, their labor generates the lion's share of our revenue. That sounds like a pretty significant stakeholder group to me. I can't help but mention how uncomfortable it feels for me to hear you refer to it as a 'thing.' It's an issue. It's a big issue. Black lives matter.

"Which is actually the second part of my point. Not acknowledging what's going on and being silent is actually making a statement because we take a position on other issues that impact us politically, environmentally, and financially. So when we deny our employees the acknowledgment that we care about something as fundamental as this, we send a message that challenges the website rhetoric."

Susan interrupted, "I'm sorry. I didn't mean to imply that it isn't important. I should have used another word."

"No problem, Susan. Thank you for the apology. I realize that it wasn't deliberate, but that is actually a good example of why we need to get more comfortable with productive dialogue about race at work. My next point is that I could probably save us the time, discretionary effort, and dollar value of the number of hours that a task force will spend on what you are proposing." LaToya grabbed a napkin and wrote: "Culture eats strategy for breakfast."

Susan replied, "I don't understand."

"Our culture and practice of tolerating—and in some cases, promoting—a good ole boy network is eating our strategy of capitalizing on the business case for diversity. Every day, all over the company, decisions are being made from unconscious bias, and people are afraid to call it out for fear of career suicide. Honestly, I'm part of the problem because I don't go to HR with every example I see. Quite frankly, I wouldn't even be having this conversation if you hadn't approached me today. I just don't have the confidence that the months of extra hours we would all put in would yield any real results unless we get serious about changing our culture around inclusion. If we decide to do that, and create a different assignment, I'm in. We need an approach to help us combine change management and leadership development that is focused on all of the levers that will create real change. We will probably need outside consultants to help us. You know how we don't believe anything until we pay $500 an hour to hear it.

"My last thought is that I recommend you select a very senior white male to lead this task force. It will give him the insight and development he needs to share this message with his peers. Having a white male on this engagement with bonus money hanging in the balance is the key to making progress."

Susan sat silent for a moment. She appreciated LaToya's candor but needed a minute to recover from what she'd just heard.

When LaToya got home, she poured a glass of wine and looked at her cell phone. She was emotionally spent and knew she needed more than wine. She wondered what was taking Shane so long. It had taken her years to realize that the poker face often required at work did not serve her intimate relationships. What her man needed most was her trust in him that her vulnerability would not be betrayed. When they surrendered their weaknesses to each other, it gave them both power to be even stronger. She couldn't resist anymore. "#911 #ineedahug," and she pressed Send.

Within thirty minutes, Shane appeared at her door with carryout and two bottles of her favorite red wine. LaToya closed the door and fell into his arms. He knew his role from this moment forward was to hold her, be her comfort, and restore the pieces of her soul she'd given to Susan. The depth of their love for each other and longevity of their relationship made him uniquely qualified for this assignment. He was the thunder, and she was the lightning. Together they could create or weather any storm.

STATEMENT №3

That night, Susan had an unusually long debrief about her day at work. Her husband, Jim, was an active listener, and they often worked through their career challenges together.

Susan replayed her conversation with LaToya and waited patiently for Jim to express his disbelief at LaToya's decision. Instead, he said, "Makes sense," and continued taking off his clothes as if this was the most normal thing he had ever heard.

"What part of turning down a major career opportunity makes sense to you?" Susan questioned.

"Come on, Susan. Sounds like LaToya walked you through it pretty clearly. What part don't you get?" Jim knew his wife may have needed him to have a different response, but he didn't have the emotional energy to provide anything but the truth after the long day he'd had.

"I understand that this stuff is stressful for Black people, but we aren't going to change a whole society overnight. This task force is a big step in the right direction to make a lasting impact for the company and all of its employees." Susan was still shocked that she had to explain so much of this to her husband.

"Okay. Honey, I get where you're coming from, but at the risk of sounding like an unsupportive jerk of a husband, I think you're missing the core issue. First of all, this 'stuff' is obviously life and death for African Americans. Secondly, lots of things in today's society change overnight—why not racism in corporate America? Hell, the LGBT community got domestic partner benefits while the religious community was still opposing same-sex relationships. Why can't we equalize the talent gap fifty years after the Civil Rights Movement?" Jim left the question hanging and waited for a response that he knew could turn into a full-blown argument. Susan said nothing, so he made an attempt to close the loop and get to bed.

"Sweetie, we aren't going to solve this tonight either. But the best thing that we can do is to begin to stretch our understanding of what this must feel like and start doing the things that will make a difference. It sounds like LaToya gave you some insight that you can take back to your department and really make a difference with." Jim continued as a memory surfaced. "I had a similar experience a few weeks ago when I overheard a group of African Americans talking about their experience. As painful as it was to hear, it prompted me to take a closer look at my own assumptions, at some of the ways our company operates and how that might impact people of color. We just started the process, and I am already excited about what kind of real change this can start."

Jim continued, "I have shifted the way I see a lot of these issues. I have engaged my leadership team in real dialogue, and I am pushing them to think about our approaches differently. Ultimately, I'm going to hold them accountable for different results, but dialogue is the first step. I have started following a few thought leaders online. Roland Martin, for example: I like how he understands corporate challenges and holds people accountable. On one of his TV shows they addressed the fact that people often bring up Black-on-Black crime as if it justifies police brutality. It doesn't. If a Black man kills another Black man, he will go to jail. If he kills (or maybe even is suspected of killing) a white person, he goes under the jail. If a police officer is caught on video with six witnesses, he may not be charged, much less go to jail. We have to be willing to address those kinds of disparities in our justice system."

"I never thought of it that way," Susan replied quietly.

Jim continued, "Another example. How many times have you heard the business case for diversity?"

"Tons of times. It is a great place to start the conversation about why these issues are important. It is especially important to get senior leaders' attention. Why do you ask?" Susan asked reluctantly.

"I'm just wondering if it isn't doing more harm than good," Jim replied, sounding less confident than he had before. After a moment's pause, he continued. "I asked our HR department to take a closer look at our talent strategy overall and diversity in particular. Our chief human resources officer started the conversation with the business case for diversity and went on to explain all of the reasons why diverse ideas impact the bottom line. He talked about things like customer connection and being able to demonstrate that we understand our customer base and innovation, about gaining value from different kinds of ideas and how that gets us to better solutions. As I was sitting there, it dawned on me—have you ever heard of the business case for white males? Sounds crazy, right? Just think of the insult that is embedded in that theory. We have to justify why it is good business practice to hire people of color. But it never occurs to us to justify why we hire white males. Our expertise and value toward our business goals of innovation, customer connection, and everything else are assumed. If we were truly hiring objectively using the tools and practices we already have, the business case for diversity would become irrelevant because everyone's contribution would be based on their credentials and an unbiased interview that led us to objective hiring and promotion decisions.

"So I have asked for an independent talent audit. I have someone coming in to help us figure out why our promotion numbers for people of color are so low and our attrition rates are so high. We do an okay job of hiring based on the available labor pool, but somehow this segment of our employee base isn't being promoted, and ultimately, they are leaving faster than we recruit them. I need to understand more about that. So I'm treating it like any other business trend that is a threat to our success."

Jim adjusted the pillow on his side of the bed. "Let's just be real. Inequities exist. I didn't create them, but as a man of conscience in a position of power, I can help to correct them. I can't make everything right, but I can make a difference. As white people, our voices matter, and we have to put aside our guilt and be a part of the solution. On the flip side, our silence is an endorsement statement that we are okay with the status quo. And I am not. Not because it is good business but because it is good humanity."

Jim waited for at least a nonverbal acknowledgment that they could switch gears back to being husband and wife. Susan looked at him and put her head on his shoulder like a traditional damsel in distress. He kissed her on the forehead, took her by the hand, and led her to bed.

STATEMENT №4

Elijah had never canceled a Happy Hour Happening, but today every fiber of his being was demanding he stay in bed. He felt guilty about missing work but later convinced himself that sick days were allocated for times such as these. He had to admit that there was a part of him that worried about the stigma of being labeled as lazy, despite the years of good examples he had provided at the firm. He was fine yesterday but couldn't move today.

His friends were dialing and texting to check on him—it seemed like every hour on the hour. He reached over to answer the phone. "Hi, Maya. Yeah, I'm gonna be aight. For real. Yes, I'm taking the stuff from the health food store. And I will call you if I need anything." Maya had to be the most nurturing personality of all the women he knew, and while he appreciated her concern, what Elijah wanted more than anything was to be cared for and comforted by his partner, not a woman.

There was something about being sick and home alone that caused him to reflect on the reality of being a gay Black man in the closet fifteen years after his divorce. As far as everyone was concerned, he was a middle-aged divorcé living the all-star-bachelor life. And that's what he wanted them to think. He was sure to be seen at events with women and very often chose to take Natasha, who held the title of Main Squeeze. But below the pretense, he was tired of living a lie. His heart ached for the love expressed by a man to another man—specifically love from Nathan.

Nathan was also African American, divorced, and in the closet. Their relationship met the mutual need for secrecy in public and intimacy in private. They each possessed the balanced qualities of strength and nurturing that the other needed. Their hearts ached for each other when they were apart and provided comfort like a newborn baby on breast milk when they were together.

Soon after Nathan arrived with chicken noodle soup, tissues, and Robitussin, Elijah launched a familiar conversation. "Now that gay marriage is legal nationwide, maybe it's time for us to come out."

Nathan took an extra second before answering. "Isn't it hard enough to be a Black man in America? Why would I compound my life to be a gay Black man? No, thank you. I'm okay living this lie until I am independently wealthy and don't need society and its judgment to make a living. This ruling doesn't change anything for us. I will support you if you want to come out, but I'm not ready yet."

Elijah grasped for another key point. "Gay rights are the new civil rights. Isn't it worth fighting for?"

"Please don't tell me you been drinking that Kool-Aid. I wish I could get the input of an ancestor who was hung from a tree to weigh in on how stupid that shit sounds. How can you compare sexual orientation to racial discrimination? Although I didn't choose my sexual orientation, I can choose to live in the closet for the rest of my life if I decide to. Can I choose to show up in this world as a

Black man? Rachel Dolezal, the former NAACP chapter president, was crucified for perpetrating because no one wants the reverse to be true. God forbid the light-skinned brothers and sisters start passing as white. That would upset the equilibrium. So how in the world can it be the same thing when choice lies at the crux of the issue? They need to keep those two separate."

Elijah sighed and said, "Don't you want to live as the best version of yourself?"

"Oh, Lord. Please, Eli. I'm not in the mood for Oprah reruns." Nathan stopped him in his tracks and spoke his peace. "This is the best version of myself I can manage at this point. Frankly, my soul can't handle any more pain, any more ridicule, any more brutality. I hurt for our boys being killed on the street and our men being overlooked for promotions in favor of every other diverse candidate. Truth be told, I simply can't take anymore. Showing up every day as a heterosexual male allows me to operate as close to normal as I can. I don't want to be ostracized any further. My silence about being gay is a statement that my authentic self is simply too painful in America."

Eli knew he wasn't going to change Nathan's mind, and it was no use trying. This complicated issue needed to get filed away with the myriad other complicated issues that Black men faced. And the façade would continue. Back to regularly scheduled programming.

Eli picked up his phone. "Hi, Natasha. It's Eli." The two exchanged the normal small talk, and then he asked, "What are you doing on Saturday the thirteenth? Okay, good. Do you want to go to the ABC Gala with me?"

5

THE REVELATION

Just as Roshunda was getting organized for the day, her coworker arrived at her desk. "So what do you think about the trouble Bill Cosby is in?"

I don't know Bill Cosby, motherfucker. But I know that you didn't have any questions for me when that crazy son of a bitch killed nine people in a church in South Carolina. So get your ass outta my face before I smack you.

In an instant, Roshunda heard her politically correct alter ego say, "I don't know Bill Cosby. But I couldn't help but wonder what does Heathcliff Huxtable have to do with what he did? Why did his show get taken out of syndication? And why didn't Charlie Sheen get taken off the air for his disgusting behavior with women? Do you have any insight on that?" Her brain had just had one of those massively disjointed moments when the answer she really wanted to say played in stereo in her head before her mouth generated an appropriate response. In that moment she realized just how exhausting the entire process was, and she had an instant headache.

It occurred to Roshunda that no one in the office had expressed any sentiment after the massacre in South Carolina. All of a sudden, she felt the pain that their silence brought when she realized that even something so horrific wouldn't move them to express compassion for her community. She was reminded of a line from Wes Moore's book *The Work*. He told a story of arriving at Oxford as a Rhodes scholar in the weeks after 9/11. As his international colleagues greeted him, they offered their sympathy over what happened. "The messages were simple, moving expressions of our shared humanity," he called it.

If this was possible from strangers or people he had just met, for Roshunda it felt like a reminder that silence is indeed a statement that contradicts the rhetoric about race in the workplace. To add insult to injury, the thought that someone would engage her in conversation about something like that was completely offensive in the absence of any other conversation about current events. Meanwhile, the asshole who'd started the conversation was probably thinking that he was doing what he learned in diversity training—striking up a conversation with someone different from him. Her question about Charlie Sheen may not have even landed in the learning space that she intended it to. It probably went right over his head. And he possibly walked away with the impression that Roshunda was yet another angry Black woman who defended what is clearly unacceptable behavior. In fact, what she was really angry about was that generations of young people could be denied the positive impact that *The Cosby Show* had on her and her parents' generations.

It had been a while since the gang had gathered for drinks. The camaraderie and conversation were well overdue. So much had happened in the world and in each of their lives. Roshunda needed an outlet, but she wasn't looking forward to hearing "I told you so" as she shared her impressions of her recent experiences at work. After three years of challenging LaToya's views, she finally felt like she understood her radical position on race in the workplace.

Eli greeted her first and looked like he had the weight of the world on his shoulders. Something was wrong, but she knew that this wasn't the time to find out what it was. Shane was his normal sexy self. She made a note to herself to stop fantasizing about him. At some point she would have to accept that he and LaToya had an addiction to each other that meant she could only ever be a side chick.

Maya was bubbly and motherly as usual. Roshunda felt so nurtured in her presence. She was relieved that LaToya wasn't there yet. Maybe she could tell her story and get some much-needed comfort from the others before Miss Know-It-All blew in.

After the essential pleasantries were exchanged, Roshunda couldn't hold her peace anymore. "Okay, you guys, I get it. I think I finally get what you all have been talking about all these years. Corporate America is not a level playing field."

"That's your news flash, Roshunda? Really? What brought you to this stark revelation?" Eli said in an uncharacteristically sarcastic tone.

"I was given a special assignment to be part of an interviewing panel for this year's intern program. We must have talked to 250 candidates to fill thirty-six roles. I got to meet and interact with about fifty-five leaders that I wouldn't have met otherwise. It was an eye-opening experience. I feel like my naivete was snatched from my heart and replaced with cynicism.

"These folks do some crazy stuff that I never really noticed before. For example, a white candidate would come in, and the hiring manager would be all warm and fuzzy. Offering them water, asking about the commute in and making small talk. I never realized how important this time is to help get your thoughts together and feel comfortable. And then when an African American or Hispanic candidate came in, they would be more matter of fact, straight to the point and start firing off questions right away. Then during the conversation they would go off script from the behavioral interview questions we are supposed to be asking. Instead of sticking to "Tell me about a time when …" they would give away key elements that we are looking for and then say, "Do you have any experience in this area?" So of course the candidate could position any old example to meet our need. I'm watching this shit and shaking my head. And after the interview, it was interesting to hear how they interpreted what they heard from candidates. They overinflated the white candidates' experience and undermined the other examples they heard. I couldn't believe how impressed they were with a day-long nonprofit event that a white boy coordinated. Meanwhile they didn't even seem to hear another example where a sister spent the summer delivering babies in a medical clinic in Tanzania. Unbelievable.

"I guess what struck me the most is the blind spot from which they operate. They have no idea that they are doing these things, and I'm sure if someone pointed it out they would deny it to the end. But it is so obvious to observe."

Roshunda continued. "I can't help but wonder, If we continue to need a hashtag for #blacklivesmatter and continue to have examples that they don't—#trayvonmartin, #ericgardner, #michaelbrown, #walterscott, #sandrabland—then how does that phenomenon inadvertently minimize the value of Black candidates in the workplace? If our lives don't matter on the main streets of America, then our impact on Wall Street could be minimized."

Everyone sat in silence for a moment. Roshunda had just channeled Freudian theory, and no one could argue with the rationale of her question. She broke the awkward silence by continuing. "If we were focusing equally and appropriately on the candidates' credentials, then the business case for D&I would be irrelevant. Everyone's impact on the bottom line would be equalized by the fact that we recruit and hire for the right skills and develop people objectively when they get here. This whole experience got me really intrigued by HR and everything it does. I had lunch with a guy from talent management. I learned a ton about HR and how that function has changed in the past few years. I shared my observations, and he sounded happy to have the feedback. He asked if I would be willing to talk with some consultants they have who are doing interviews about our HR processes. I have a follow-up conversation with them next week. I don't understand exactly what it's all about, but it sounds exciting. And I think I kinda like this HR stuff."

Maya stepped in to give Roshunda the kudos she knew her generation needed. "Well done, my dear. Those are very insightful observations, especially considering that you started from a place of skepticism. I love how you got on this assignment, made your observations, and then took them to the right person. That was a bold move and risky spending of career equity—but it looks like it worked out. Hopefully the company takes advantage of your insight. In the meantime, document all this stuff. Just in case anything funny starts happening, you'll want to have a paper trail for potential retaliation."

"Thanks, Maya. I appreciate you. I know it has been hard to love me through my hardheadedness." They exchanged hugs, and everyone felt the love between them.

6

JIM MOVES TO ACTION

As Jim approached his fifty-fifth birthday, he could feel himself becoming more introspective. It seemed like a natural phenomenon to start thinking about the important things in life. What did he want his legacy to be? He was clear about his family life, but what about at work and in the community? What did he want to be remembered for? Had he achieved his life's purpose? Was there really such a thing? Or do we decide what we want to achieve in the world and create our own version of purpose?

Jim was not a religious person and often wondered how generations of people could believe in doctrines based on texts from thousands of years ago that had so many inherent inconsistencies and contradictions. But lately he found himself craving for the sense of peace that a belief in religion offered. He knew that somehow the Universe was moving him to a new way of thinking through seemingly coincidental experiences that altered how he thought about race in the workplace.

First, it was the conversation he'd overheard in the restaurant. Then there was his debrief with Susan after her conversation with LaToya. And most recently, the president of their African American employee resource group had sent him a video by Matthew Cooke that shook his understanding of white privilege and the history behind the challenges America was facing. All of a sudden, he felt like he got it. He understood what felt like years of contempt for white males and the corresponding guilt they felt about their success. All of a sudden, he wondered how all this had impacted his decisions as a leader throughout his career. And, more importantly, what could he do about it now?

Jim didn't have all the answers, nor did he pretend to. But what he had was legitimate power and authority in the organization to create change and establish policies and systems to sustain its impact. He gave his leadership team two assignments as prework for the upcoming off-site meeting: the Matthew Cooke video and a *Harvard Business Review* article by Muriel Maignan Wilkins titled "Why Executives Should Talk about Racial Bias at Work."

After all his research, pondering alone, conversations with other CEOs, and listening in—it was time to move to action.

"Good morning, ladies and gentlemen." Jim's leadership team knew that this was no ordinary off-site. Each of them had been collecting data, running reports, and serving at the beck and call of the consultants brought in to do the talent audit. They resented the feeling of being audited and couldn't help being anxious about what the findings would be. Many of them could predict that the bottom-line outcomes would be dismal in terms of minority hiring and promotion. Their biggest fear was that no one had an explanation that would make any sense at this point.

"Thank you all very much for the extra work that this audit has required of you and for making time for the prework I sent. I also appreciate Jasmine and her team of consultants for organizing the work to facilitate the data collection and for helping us to coordinate the various approaches we will be using. Let's begin with the end in mind. As I stated a few months ago, my intention with this initiative is to take a deep dive on what role, if any, race plays in the execution of our talent strategy. I think I told you how this all came about. Imagine you are sitting in a restaurant and you happen to overhear a group of strangers talk about what it feels like to be a person of color inside an organization. I couldn't help but wonder what our employees might say in the same setting. As difficult as it was to hear, it was an incredible gift of insight that I have grown from. Many of you questioned the narrow focus on race and wondered why women and other diverse groups were not included.

"Four considerations:

1. This was an additional initiative that wasn't budgeted for. So in the absence of an unlimited budget, we have to focus our efforts. We have several initiatives in flight for women. But we have never had a dedicated focus on people of color.

2. We are being irresponsible with our human resources if we are not leveraging 100 percent of our employees' potential. If we are paying people and not creating an environment for them to maximize their participation, then we are leaving money on the table, wasting time, and inviting our competitors to eat our lunch.

3. When you consider that what we call 'human resources' are actually people, let's look at it this way. Based on what I have been seeing in the news, there is an urgent need to focus on the population impacted by generations of segregation and current-day police brutality. I see this as part of our values around community responsibility. Some of the problems in our communities are economic problems. Day-to-day decisions in families and communities are based on the employment income that they have access to.

So I want to make sure that 100 percent of our employees have an equal opportunity to make the best decisions that they can afford for their families.

4. We will take a deep dive on other populations at a later date. Just not right now.

"Any questions on that?" Jim waited a moment. "Okay. My intention here is to

a. find out if we are leveraging 100 percent of the talent available in the market and in our company;
b. find out how we are doing that or why we aren't; and
c. establish new policies, procedures, and a corresponding culture that will change that in the short term and sustain it in the long term.

"Our process was to conduct a talent audit that looked at

a. candidates sourced, interviewed, and hired compared to the relative percentage of those hired;
b. promotion and development rates of people of color relative to white males;
c. compensation differences between people of color and white males and females; and
d. organizational culture issues that may be impacting the results above.

"Today, we will hear those results, understand the implications, and begin brainstorming solutions. Any questions?"

Jim had extraordinary range in his leadership style. He was an ideal role model for situational leadership, emotional intelligence, and managerial courage. He understood what this moment called for and nailed it.

Jasmine had been working closely with Jim, his leadership team, and the HR business partners for almost four months. She had a unique combination of internal and external corporate experience that gave her a distinct advantage with this work. She had become known for leveraging her strengths to connect disparate dots that others didn't see and to identify past trends and potential challenges that others simply missed.

She began her overview. "This is not a recap of diversity scorecard metrics that you have seen many times before. This is a deep dive down one particular path. How do people of color experience your organization?"

She then recapped the methodology used and delivered the results in seventeen minutes flat. It felt more like a military operation than the normal consultant intellectualization. Just the facts, no filler. Although no one was shocked by the disparities, there was a sense of collective embarrassment over seeing the findings projected in front of them in black and white, literally and figuratively.

"In essence," Jasmine said, "our findings indicate that we have been sourcing from the same handful of colleges and universities for some time, with a distinct preference for hiring from manager alma mater institutions.

- We have four of 886 hires in the last two years who were from HBCUs.

- Of the twenty-four people of color (POC) hired in the last two years, 85 percent were overqualified for the roles they were brought into. In six cases, higher-level positions were available—but not explored for those candidates.

- The promotion rate for white males in the company is 3.65 years. The corresponding promotion rate for people of color is 8.75 years.

- The differentiated talent strategy adopted seven years ago has intensified this gap. All efforts and spending were diverted to identifying and investing in high-potential candidates. By forcing the organization to compete against itself, nomination trends tended to follow the hiring trends, which tended to mirror the existing population of white males.

- It seems to me that the way you are executing the differentiated talent strategy either creates or perpetuates a 'haves and have nots' system inside the company. This strategy has inherent challenges, given the realities of unconscious bias.

- Leadership development programs were targeted for high-potential employees only. The participant population of leadership development programs was 73 percent white male, 16 percent white female, 4 percent males of color, and 7 percent females of color. There is a gap in males of color being identified as 'hi-pos,' or high-potential employees.

- Ninety percent of 'ready now' candidates are white. Ten percent are POC. Forty-two percent of 'ready in three to five years' candidates are POC. Fifteen people have been rated 'ready now' or 'ready in one to two years' for five years plus and were never offered a new role.

- Eighty-five percent of top-rated performers—4.5 to 5—are white. Fifteen percent are people of color.

- With respect to salaries: starting salaries for POC were 27 percent less than that of white males, and promotion salaries were 38 percent lower than their white male counterparts.

- The anecdotal information collected during focus groups was equally alarming:

- Seven leaders were named repeatedly as being biased and/or openly racist. People seemed to know and accept their behavior. One of them was sitting in the room when the results were read.

- Mentoring seemed to be working well—for white males. There was specific mention of the meetings before and after the meetings and sidebar conversations where important information was shared off the record. This doesn't include the additional impact of lunches and after-hours invitations that seemed to be offered to the same predictable list of 'rock stars.' Similarly, reassuring glances during meetings and feedback after the meeting were also provided to some people and not others. Advocacy and sponsorship was actively being used and potential often inflated in favor of 'young protégés.' Meanwhile, people of color were often expected to demonstrate their capabilities in multiple scenarios before basic compliments and opportunities were offered.

• There was also evidence of a strong relationship culture. Ironically, people thought this approach was supporting productivity and made comments like 'We get results through relationships.' In fact, this overreliance on relationships has some unintended consequences:

a. Bad decisions were sometimes made in favor of good relationships. For example, we heard about Ralph in accounting, who apparently 'is the biggest asshole in finance, but everyone knows he is personal friends with the SVP and continues to receive opportunities that he isn't ready for.'"

Jasmine read verbatim from her notes for impact, paused, and then continued.

> b. "People often covered up errors and infractions that hinted at unethical behavior. We are not willing to say that this is occurring because no one came out with any examples during our interviews. However, based on the facial expressions and glances I saw—I'm adding it here in the 'worth looking into' column.

- There were reports of microinequities that Arin Reeves calls 'mosquito bites': 'Those annoying realities that remind those who are different that they are, in fact, different from the people who have historically been accepted, included and successful in that workplace.' In one focus group, an African American male gave an example of being asked if he had family members who were incarcerated.

- In one focus group, one woman said, 'The Serena Effect is alive and well here.' I had her explain it to me, even though everyone else seemed to understand. Apparently, she used this term to refer to the tendency to criticize even the best performers because they do not fit the profile of what success is 'supposed to look like.' Similar to the phenomenon of Serena Williams' body type and personal style being criticized after she has had superior results in theenis world. Her point was that this phenomenon, its way of thinking, and the subsequent actions taken—i.e., lower performance ratings and salary increases—happen inside your company as well.

- Fourteen up-and-coming leaders were identified as potential ambassadors for the changes that needed to be made. They had great ideas and gave us wonderful nuggets of insight into the culture and ideas for how to solve for them.

"One of those nuggets was something one person called 'The S4 Secret Solution.' Apparently a group of employees use this term when someone says something that ranges from mildly inappropriate to clearly offensive or detrimental to the culture. It is a sarcastic request that people would just 'stop saying stupid shit.'

"These folks were a combination of career experience levels, external hires, and home-grown leaders, of various ages and generational orientations. These employees seemed to have a significant amount of informal influence in the organization and personal passion for the company and how much better it could be."

Jasmine sat straight up. And although she looked like she was about to have a powerful summarizing comment, she said nothing but gazed empathetically at everyone around the table.

Jim broke the silence and asked, "Thoughts? Reactions?" He allowed them to sit in the discomfort of the moment just long enough to be relieved by his movement forward. He turned to the consultants and said, "Let's cut to the chase. What is your professional opinion about why this is occurring in our workplace?"

Jasmine shifted and then replied, "Your workplace is no different than many others across the country. I commend you for taking this bold step to identify these issues and being so forward-thinking in addressing them. We can do a more detailed analysis, but at a glance, we have come to three major conclusions:

1. Power is held by individuals whose unconscious bias leads them to the individual and collective decisions that created these results.

2. There seems to be an unwillingness to acknowledge or address the issues that challenge this way of thinking. We heard a few examples of information and suggestions from employees that address several of these issues and have been brought up in various forums, some of which went directly to HR.

3. This way of working has become an engrained and accepted part of your culture to the point that it isn't recognized by those doing it or consistently challenged by those who do recognize it. After several failed attempts, people stop making an issue for fear of covert retaliation. Others simply leave the organization.

"We took the liberty of contacting twenty-five people of color who left the organization in the past thirty-six months. They were willing to be candid with us because we explained our role as externals conducting a confidential talent audit. Their responses validated these findings. Ninety percent said that ultimately they left their boss, not the company. Overall this is a great company, but over time the culture became more than they were willing to endure for a paycheck they could receive elsewhere.

"I asked if they were happy with where they landed. Nineteen of them were. Six found that 'although the grass is greener, the manure smells the same.' One person specifically got the promotion she felt was impossible here and is making more money, but some of the same microinequities exist. I asked all of them if they would consider reemployment here. Only that one who gave the example would do so, and only on the condition that she could be part of a solution to change the culture."

"And what do you recommend we do about this?" Jim probed.

"First of all, let's clarify that this is at least a two-pronged approach.

1. The actions that you take immediately, and
2. more importantly, the culture you create over time.

"I highly recommend a full-blown intervention managed like any other campaign that you expect bottom-line, tangible results from. This intervention must include both of those focus areas.

"You need

- a tangible, quantifiable goal;

- a clear plan for how you will achieve this—you must be willing to do things differently and say out loud what you're doing;

- specialized resources dedicated to focusing on this (adding it to someone's existing job won't work);

- strong program management with informal influence and formal authority to coordinate the elements and lead through the challenges that this initiative brings;

- a change management strategy to guide the messages, timing, and overall execution;

- a communication plan that can be tweaked as necessary; and

- a willingness to adjust as necessary."

Jasmine took a breath, then continued. "We have targeted resources for each of these elements wrapped in a model we call DARE:

- Decide that you are serious about this transformation, and then just do it.

- Allocate the resources—time and money—to do it, and hold people accountable for the process and the results.

- Review and revamp existing policies, procedures, systems, and people who are operating contrary to the future state you want.

- Execute the changes required, and evaluate the results on an ongoing basis.

"Our premise is that these issues are far less complicated than most companies make them out to be. The solutions aren't rocket science, but they do require an above-average amount of leadership courage and organizational commitment to address the issues you say you want to change. You are welcome to work with us or use any other firm or model that takes you from a sincere decision all the way to transforming your company and evaluating your progress long term."

"What questions do you guys have?" Jim asked.

Walter had been itching to demonstrate that he was listening in the last round of diversity training. "So have we identified the business case for this initiative? Do we have a target ROI? How will we justify this narrow focus and allocation of resources to the board? What about the change management required? Sounds like we are about to send the organization into a tailspin."

Jim waited for someone to respond. After what seemed like thirty seconds of awkward silence, Jim opened his leather portfolio and handed Walter a sheet of paper.

"Actually, Walter, I have thought about all of that. In response to your first question, I'd like you to read this out loud. It is the response that Howard Schultz, CEO of Starbucks, made to a shareholder about the company's support for homosexual marriage."

Walter cleared his throat. "Not every decision is an economic decision. Despite the fact that you recite statistics that are narrow in time, we did provide a 38 percent shareholder return over the last year. I don't know how many things you invest in, but I would suspect not many things, companies, products, investments have returned 38 percent over the last twelve months. Having said that, it is not an economic decision to me. The lens in which we are making that decision is through the lens of our people. We employ over two hundred thousand people in this company, and we want to embrace diversity—of all kinds. If you feel, respectfully, that you can get a higher return than the 38 percent you got last year, it's a free country. You can sell your shares in Starbucks and buy shares in another company. Thank you very much."

Jim said, "I agree with Howard. Although I am firmly focused on making money for this company, this is not a financial decision. You know why, Walter? Because hiring you wasn't a financial decision. We assumed that based on your experience and credentials, you were the right person for our job. Or at least we thought so when you started twenty-three years ago.

"We are going to move past this offensive 'business case for diversity' in favor of embracing an inclusive talent strategy that leverages 100 percent of our existing staff and 100 percent of the talent market's potential in support of our business goals.

"A few thoughts on this shift:

- If you still need justification or an explanation for why hiring and promoting diversity makes business sense, then this is not the company for you.

- My expectation is that these, and several other, changes in our culture will create that level playing field where every external candidate and internal promotion are evaluated exclusively and objectively based on their credentials and how effectively we think they can help us to meet our business goals. We are going to revise the HR tools used and add some oversight during the transition. We may not be resourced to do this effectively right now. We will take a step back and ask for support from our HR business partners to help us course correct. This might be the single most important strategic imperative that HR supports. Ultimately, we will be able to defend every talent decision we make. Not because anyone forces us to but because it has become part of our new culture.

"I know this is a big shift. But the reality is that we have been farting around with this for years. Hiring goes up, retention goes down. Despite the progress made by talent acquisition, we can't keep the talent we recruit, and our slates continue to look the same. It's time to do something different. This isn't intended to be an instant trans- formation. It will take us time. There are changes I expect to see immediately and results that I realize will take three to five years. The point here is that we have to get serious and start somewhere. All the gains we achieve here are transferable to other populations.

"How is this sounding to you?" Jim asked. "Thoughts? Reactions?"

Everyone sat quietly and looked to each other to rescue the moment with a comment. No one said anything.

"Okay. We will have many more opportunities to share thoughts. Right now you might be wondering, How in the world are we going to do this? Well, I have a few ideas about that as well. I have been thinking about the magnitude of the culture changes and the change management we need to ensure we stay competitive in the new economy. What we discussed today about our talent strategy is one aspect of it. There are other ways we need to change as well.

"I've been doing this for thirty-two years, and I have seen culture serve the greater good, like Southwest Airlines, and I have seen companies collapse under their own weight, like Kodak. I didn't need Ford's bankruptcy example to know that 'culture eats strategy for breakfast.' But I am grateful that they had the experience and not us. My responsibility to our shareholders, to the board, to our employees, and to our customers is to protect the current value of our company and grow the future value. Right now we are suboptimizing our workforce. If we continue this trend, we will find ourselves reorganizing the proverbial deck chairs on the *Titanic*. And I won't let that happen. Let's take a thirty-minute break and reconvene to plan our next steps."

The room emptied quickly, and Jasmine approached Jim. "I know how difficult that was. You nailed it. Today is a start, just context setting. Don't feel the need to get full buy-in. It will trickle in gradually."

During the last phase of the meeting, they reviewed what they had covered so far and dove into a few more questions about the findings. They discussed and agreed on a few guiding principles for the initiative that everyone could embrace. Jim also announced that his team would spend two full days immersed in the concept of unconscious bias. A separate firm was engaged for that training. Jasmine would continue to oversee the overall approach and coordinate the use of various consultants for specialized aspects. Her role was to help Jim and his senior leadership team to focus on building and sustaining a culture of inclusion and get to a point of maximizing 100 percent of their human capital.

Everyone filed out of the room. But Walter's commitment was still uncertain. And for the first time, everyone realized the possibility that he may not make it in the new culture. The only remaining question was whether he would come to that conclusion on his own or whether Jim would help get him there.

7

SUCCESS
BY GRACE

I f ever excitement mixed with regret could cause a queasy feeling, it was today. This was the last of the happy hour gatherings for quite a while. LaToya was moving to LA for a new VP job, and Shane had decided to go with her. Those two were finally ready to admit that the universe couldn't do without their union. They weren't sure if marriage was in the cards, but they knew they had to be together. Shane had not found a job yet, but he was willing to take his chances if it meant being with the woman he couldn't be without.

Maya was loving life. Her business was thriving, and she had several new corporate clients. She was finally seeing the benefits of being a certified minority business, and once she was given an opportunity to compete with the big boys, her business tripled. She'd bought a beach house in Miami and couldn't wait to spend her days by the ocean. She had a spectacular view from her veranda. She had finally been able to finance her soul's desire to spend her days by the seashore. Her children were at different places in their lives. Her oldest was applying for a transfer with his job that would bring him to one of their locations in Fort Lauderdale. He and his family could be closer to Grand Mia but far enough away to live their own lives.

Roshunda had just transitioned into HR. She was grateful for the opportunity to make a lateral move and do something completely different than she had ever done before. Her sales skills gained her accolades for communication, influence, and an orientation for results. Her goal was to translate those strengths and make a difference to change the complacent culture that she had come to resent at her company. Their recent initiative to change the company culture was refreshing, as she could see definite proof that they were serious. The CEO was ushering in a new season of change, and a few key executives, including a long-standing member of the executive team named Walter, had retired. She knew how significant this was, and she was excited to be part of a solution that seemed like a serious step forward.

As each of them came streaming into the bar, they exchanged hugs and kisses that seemed to last a little longer this time.

Eli was at a crossroads in his life and wasn't sure what he was going to do. He wasn't sure if he would stay in the DC area or see what life had in store for him elsewhere. He loved Nathan, and although they were committed to each other, his soul was telling him that it was time to be true to himself. He wasn't sure that he could keep this secret anymore and wondered if he needed a fresh start in a new city. He was willing, for the first time ever, to live on his own terms. "Hey, everyone. I have something to tell you," he started.

"You guys aren't gonna believe this. I'm in the final stages of interviewing for a chief supply chain officer role." Shane interrupted Eli and launched the conversation before everyone had even connected their butts to seats. "It was the craziest thing. I was at the mall, and someone shouts out, 'Thunder!' I'm thinking ... that has to be someone from way back to call me by my line name. Turns out Hunter, a white guy from college, was visiting DC for a conference and ran into the mall to get a tie. That's coincidence number one. We get to talking, and I tell him I'm moving to LA. I mentioned that I am looking for a job and I want to stay in supply chain. He tells me he just got an email about a chief supply chain officer role. He wondered why anyone would send it to him. Clearly it was meant for me. He forwarded it from his phone right there! That's coincidence number two." At this point, everyone knew how the story ended, and they were holding back the hallelujahs. "Long story short—I did a phone screen, phone interview, initial and second interviews with the entire senior leadership team. Just waiting to hear back at this point." Shane sat back and threw his hands up.

Maya grabbed Eli, Eli grabbed Roshunda, and Roshunda grabbed LaToya. LaToya grabbed Shane, and Shane grabbed Maya—all in a split second. "Father, we agree right here in this blessed moment that if this role is for Shane, he will have it. Right now, in the name of Jesus, we claim this job or something better. Whatever is your will in divine order. It is done." They all forgot they were in a public place and channeled the power of their ancestors on Shane's behalf. "Amen and ashe." They opened their eyes and continued the conversation as if the power of the Holy Ghost had not just been in their midst.

"I'm happy that everyone is making moves but I'm sad that this is gonna be our last get-together for a while. I've learned so much from all of you. I feel like you are my corporate parents who raised me in the work world," Roshunda said.

LaToya chimed in for the first time. "I know that I never woulda made it without y'all. Lord knows I had my days when I was ready to lose it behind something that someone did or said at work or something happening in or to our community. The silence of our experience can be such a heavy burden to carry. When are we going to recognize the connection between inclusion and productivity? Dialogue and innovation?"

Roshunda added, "In addition to dialogue, we need real change. We need more CEOs to understand how much talent is being wasted while the good ole boy network flourishes. I know people try to downplay the impact of being on the DiversityInc Top 50 Companies list, but there's no denying that companies that leverage 100 percent of their workforce outperform those that don't. I admire Luke Visconti; he is one of the few non-Black people willing to put himself out there to address what's wrong with our large corporations. And at least he is doing the work to offer solutions."

Shane's phone rang louder than anyone had ever heard a ringer go off. He leaped out of his seat and gave them the 'excuse me' finger used at church.

Eli brought everyone's attention back to the conversation. "LaToya, you need to let that go. You may never work for a company that has that kind of culture around race in the workplace. Your best bet is to focus on what you can do to help others. Those folks at your old job didn't know what they had."

LaToya interrupted and said, "They know now. They're blowing up my phone with a counteroffer, trying to get me to stay, offering a promotion and all the perks. I have been busting my butt for nine years. Now, all of a sudden they realize my value and want to negotiate. Don't get me wrong, I've fallen for it before, and sometimes the 'buyback' works great. But this time it's too late. Telling me I'm a hi-po now won't make a difference. Lots of companies wait until we leave to show and tell us how valuable we are. What is so hard about courting us as high performers while we're there? It's awkward to find out 'how valuable you are' under those conditions. Not to mention that 'buying back your own talent' isn't very strategic."

Eli jumped back in. "When you get to this new job, continue to do your thing. Speak up when necessary, and be an example for other brothers and sisters so that they know they can be a change agent also. When we all start speaking up, companies will listen. They can't fire all of us. We gotta stop being impressed with being the 'first and only' in a role and start reaching back to help others. And when we have some influence, use it. I love how you mentor students and make time for the ones who are trying to make it. We need to reinvest our talent in our young people. Our future hinges on their self-confidence. Mentoring them is critical. Susan L. Taylor reinvented her career from editor in chief of *Essence* magazine to founder of CARES Mentoring. There are so many opportunities to make a difference with our young people."

LaToya added, "I'm all for community service, but we have to be careful that it doesn't become the only solution. That approach in a vacuum starts to sound like they created this situation themselves. In addition to mentoring youth, let's make sure their parents have a fair chance to get jobs, development opportunities, and promotions. Another thing—when someone comes out of a correctional institution, why can't we assume that they are 'corrected'? Why do we apply double jeopardy to their lives and deny them jobs for convictions that they have already served time for? I want to see more programs that help those returning to the community and more companies willing to hire them. Some of the solutions are complicated, but some of them are simple."

Roshunda added, "The other thing we need to do is start making a statement with our spending. Rosa Parks is a hero because her defiance launched the bus boycott. The boycott worked because it cost folks money. We should teach corporations to take a stand on our behalf when necessary and boycott them when they don't. My pastor, Willie Wilson, preaches about the connection between knowing our history and using it to influence our future. He says, 'Without knowledge of the past, one has no awareness in the present.'"

"Yeah," Eli added. "We also need to transfer our spending to Black-owned businesses wherever possible and ensure that our community thrives. We need to see economic influence as the new path to overcome, and today needs to be the day."

Shane blew back into the room, bursting with excitement. "I'm in! I got the job!"

Everyone at the table responded with various versions of "Hallelujah! Thank you, Jesus. Great job. Prayer works." They could hardly contain themselves.

Finally, Shane settled down and said, "You know, this is such a powerful lesson. It feels like success by grace." Everyone knew exactly what he meant but just sat quietly to let him explain. "Although our accomplishments came from hard work, sleepless nights, and putting up with our share of bullshit, if we're honest with ourselves, a large part of our success has occurred by grace. In spite of others who didn't want us to make it and/or in spite of our own mistakes and detours along the way. We weren't always on the right path. We may have chosen the wrong major in college or didn't go at all. Sometimes I didn't trust my instincts and delayed my blessing. I made some mistakes, but when I was given an opportunity to fail forward, I learned from them. We had people who crossed our paths and saw something in us that we didn't see in ourselves. Angels were conspiring on the other side to lead us to our greater good. By the grace of God, through coincidences arranged on our behalf, divine guidance led us to the right decisions and some outcomes we still can't explain."

Everyone nodded and raised their glasses for a toast. "Cheers to the next chapter."

PART II

8

APPROACHING AWKWARD CONVERSATIONS ABOUT RACE

LaToya was enjoying the feeling of starting over, both figuratively and literally. She and Shane had taken this opportunity to renegotiate a new way of living and loving each other. House hunting was fun, and decorating their new space was much more of a bonding experience than she would ever have imagined. LaToya found random opportunities to thank Shane for the sacrifices he was willing to make. She did not take it for granted that he had decided to follow her to Los Angeles before his job offer had come through. They seemed to renew their commitment to each other without rings or formality. Even though there was an unspoken depth of understanding between them, she made a conscious effort to verbalize her gratitude and demonstrate her appreciation. In return, her man showered her with love and admiration. Life was good, and love was better.

Her new company had put on the full-court press to recruit and retain her from the very beginning. LaToya saw signs that indicated this was a genuine part of how they did business, but she was also enough of a realist to know that it could be part of the D&I PR campaign. During the onboarding process, she had developed a very good relationship with her HR contact. She'd asked a lot of pointed questions about the company culture, especially as it related to diversity. Ever since her conversation with Susan, her soul had decided that she was a change agent and it would not tolerate any environment that compromised her beliefs. She had become more vocal about her views and started blogging her ideas as a cathartic way to process what she was feeling. She had been transparent with her new employer from day one. They were aware of her passion to be part of a new conversation about race in the workplace. She knew that if she became a nuisance, they could get rid of her. They knew that in the meantime they could extract value from her experience and willingness to share. Their request for her to share any insight that could help them to grow in this area seemed sincere. And even if it wasn't, LaToya was determined to behave as if it was.

"Let's go see your new office." Cheryl moved through the hallway like it was Christmastime at the mall. "We selected a choice location for you and left a few opportunities for you to decorate. Hold on one second while I make a stop." Cheryl ducked into a well-appointed office with a great view. There were boxes all over, as if someone was moving in or out. LaToya's first instinct was a bit of disappointment that this wasn't her office, because something felt familiar about it. They continued down a long hallway to what seemed like the other end of the building, turned the corner, and seemed to step into a time warp. This section of the office seemed to be a more fancy part of the building, and she saw large nostalgic portraits of former company presidents and chairmen of the board hanging on the wall. "Here we are." Cheryl grinned as they entered an oversize office with huge perpendicular windows.

"It's nice. Actually, it's beautiful. Thank you very much." LaToya put on her poker face and struggled to find a response that matched

Cheryl's excitement. They had obviously put a lot of thought and care into selecting this office for her, and she did not want to sound ungrateful. However, this space did not resonate with her. It seemed sterile, and she felt like an instant outsider.

Cheryl proceeded to give a few more instructions that seemed important, but LaToya missed most of it. She snapped out of it just in time to hear Cheryl say, "And then Eric, Jonathan, and Brad are taking you to lunch at 12:30 p.m. They wanted to be the first to welcome you. Mona, your assistant, will be here shortly. There is one little catch: she sits a little ways down the hall from you, but it's a small price to pay for the prime real estate you have here."

LaToya smiled, knowing that there was something to double-click on; she just couldn't put her finger on it—yet.

Shane was away on his first business trip and was still on cloud nine about his new job. When he and LaToya spoke that night, he had so much to share. "Babe, today was incredible. They arranged for me to have lunch with Troy; he's a brother who has been with the company for twenty-three years. This dude is EVP of the North American division, and I hear he is next in line to be CEO. I was so excited. I could hardly contain myself but still trying to act cool, you know." Shane let out a belly laugh that reminded her of reason number two hundred and nineteen why she loved him. He truly loved to see others succeed, and it seemed like his new company gave him a lot to be proud of.

"He spent time getting to know me, asking about my military and college experience and family—in a caring way. And he was just as able to send a strong message that they are about business. They have a laser focus on results, and they aren't afraid to hold people accountable. We are expected to treat our team right and get the very best out of them.

I love it." Shane seemed to be beaming. LaToya understood that her role was to listen and create the space for him to keep talking. "He told me that the executive team was very impressed with my background and how much they were looking forward to what I will bring to the company. You know, as soon as he said that, I thought back to Jane Elliott's blue-eyes, brown-eyes experiment. It makes such a difference to know that people expect the best from you. I feel like I'm starting off as a hi-po, and I'm even more motivated to prove them right."

They ended the conversation with their standard "I miss you, I miss you more, can't wait to get home" bedtime conversation.

After hearing how happy her man was, LaToya was finally ready to buckle down and finish her next blog post.

APPROACHING AWKWARD CONVERSATIONS ABOUT RACE
BY LATOYA BURGUNDY

I see two important phenomena happening simultaneously. First, there are a growing number of cases of heart-wrenching and racially charged incidences occurring with increasing regularity all over the country. Meanwhile, more time, money, and discretionary efforts are being spent on diversity and inclusion goals, initiatives, and metrics inside organizations.

Diverse groups gather in the workplace each morning and make small talk about sports events, current events, world events—and leave an obvious void around issues that appear to be racially charged or too risky to discuss at work. We assume that the silence goes unnoticed and serves the higher purpose of maintaining relationships. After all, we have been socialized not to discuss certain things in mixed company, including politics and religion. However, if the Pope visits your city and you have a coworker who is openly Catholic and was absent that day, is it okay to ask, "Did you attend the papal festivities?" I'd say yes, certainly. Relationship equity can be built by making the connection between something that is important to them and something that is also current in the news.

When the tsunami hit and thousands of people died in the Philippines, was it okay to ask a Filipino coworker, "Have you been able to contact your family members?" Again, I think so for the same reasons as above.

If there is a case of injustice in the news or a mass murder in a church, is it okay to say, "That was terrible, wasn't it?" Yes, it is.

Some might argue that you shouldn't bring up police brutality or injustice with an African American coworker. And in some cases that is absolutely true; you shouldn't. However, the example above didn't reference racism or the Confederate flag or the individual himself. It was a simple expression of shared humanity, care, and concern from one to another.

So the textbook diversity answer to the question "Should you talk about race in the workplace?" is "It depends." What is the context of the conversation? What kind of relationship do you already have or have the opportunity to build? Does the individual want to talk about it? Do they want to talk about it with *you*?

The goal is to create the space that increases our ability to share this important element of ourselves and our experience with others.

Dr. Arin Reeves, author of *One Size Never Fits All*, says, "How can we possibly be expected to deal with differences adequately in the workplace when we cannot even really talk about the ways in which differences are influencing the most intense of current events around us?"

I would go a step further to say that the conversations we aren't having are costing us trust, collaboration, and innovation. It is time to break the silence and explore how race is experienced in the workplace by African Americans, the unintended consequences of a lack of honest dialogue, and solutions that can move employees and organizations forward.

Based on my experience with employee and leadership development, I have identified four approaches that help foster dialogue and improve relationships. Over time, they also shift organizational culture in support of inclusion goals and business results.

1. Seek first to understand

    Each of us experiences life from our unique viewpoint. The ability to empathize is key to understanding how other people see the world. We all have specific causes that matter to us based on our experiences. It is easy to empathize with someone who is passionate about early detection and finding a cure for cancer. We understand that their participation in a breast cancer walk does not negate the need for or impact of the AIDS awareness campaign. Similarly, the claim that #alllivesmatter can be seen as an attempt to dismiss the impact and severity of recent incidents of police brutality that launched the #blacklivesmatter movement. Not understanding this fundamental premise can come across as holding a double standard that people expect you to understand intuitively.

Exercise empathy about experiences outside your own. Recognize nonverbal clues that indicate that what you said or did may not have landed the way you intended. Apologize quickly and sincerely if you think you may have offended someone. Your vulnerability will be appreciated.

2. Be willing to engage and be vulnerable in conversations

   Sometimes what isn't said speaks louder than words expressed. If you feel that a situation calls for something but you do not know what to say, then say that. Verbalizing a loss for words can sometimes fill a void more effectively than silence. Be willing to show your humanity at work so that others may see your whole self and be encouraged to show theirs.

3. Accept responsibility to be part of the solution

   None of us personally created the challenges our society faces today. Nor did we damage the rainforest or pollute the oceans. However, we participate in recycling efforts because we see a clear connection between the small role we play and the larger solution for a future we may not live to see. The same is true of the challenge to heal the strained relations between Black and white people in America. None of us created the dynamic that exists now, but we all have a shared responsibility in the solution that generations after us will need.

4. Approach each conversation as if it were a plastic bottle

   The choice you make to throw it away or recycle it will either damage or build the environment of trust and all of the positive benefits that come with it.

LaToya reread her work, clicked the Post button, and began reviewing the comments from her previous articles. She was beginning to get quite a following of people who loved her ideas and welcomed the candor she offered. Others were clearly not ready to address this issue and accused her of "setting race relations back one hundred years." She had made peace with her critics by remembering that powerful women are rarely popular. LaToya replied to the new comments posted, closed her laptop, grabbed the pillow, and dreamed about Shane's welcome-home celebration tomorrow night.

9

PLANNING YOUR CAREER

R oshunda was loving her new role in HR. Her mentor from talent management was such a strong supporter that the transition from sales had been smoother than she thought it would be. She had a lot to learn, and many days she gained a new understanding of what "drinking from a fire hose" really meant. She found herself working long hours, checking and even replying to WOA emails after 9:00 p.m.—but loving every minute of it. She missed sharing her learnings with the Happy Hour Posse, so she was excited about tonight's dinner, which seemed long overdue.

Before she left the office, she intended to finish the training she was writing for the Affinity Group professional development summit. She had been asked to present on the importance of career planning and had to develop three hours of content. Roshunda knew she was a credible witness, having just made a major career move herself. But she hadn't expected that putting her thoughts together would be so difficult. She really wanted to at least finish her brain dump before she left. She glanced at her phone and realized she was almost late. It would have to wait until she got back.

Eli arrived first, as usual, and was sitting in a booth, waiting. "Hello, my dear," Roshunda said in a loud voice that seemed to startle him.

"What's up, girl!" he answered. "It's great to see you."

"You too. I've been so busy with this new job. Thanks for reaching out to get this on the calendar. I've missed you and the others. I even find myself missing Miss Know-It-All." Roshunda chuckled and felt the range of the love-hate relationship between her and LaToya. The secret they kept was a heavy burden to bear, but she had to find a way to put it behind her. The affair with Shane was a distant memory. She knew he loved her, but he loved LaToya more, and forever. All she could ever be was a side chick to him. LaToya knew about what happened between them and had written it off as a fling that would never happen again. She had made a conscious decision that all three of them would coexist as friends and she would maintain her role as Shane's woman. Roshunda silently agreed, and the arrangement worked well as long as she stayed in her lane.

"I have something to ..." Roshunda's phone rang, and it was Maya. Her face lit up with excitement, and she answered quickly. "It's Maya! ... Hello? ... Hey, girl! I can't believe you're calling me this minute. I'm in our favorite booth with Eli! ... Yes, we're having dinner. Let me put you on speaker."

Maya was excited to have a chance to talk to them both. They spent the next twenty minutes catching up on each other's lives and reminiscing about old times. It had only been nine months since they'd been together last, but it felt like way longer than that.

When they got off the phone, Eli felt exhausted. There was something about being around these women that made him feel tired. The courage he thought he'd had to talk to Roshunda about his dilemma with Nathan was gone. All he could do now was listen to her updates and plan to schedule dates to fly out to LA and connect with Shane.

He made it through dinner. They hugged and said their goodbyes, and they both knew that things just weren't the same.

When Roshunda got home, she took a quick shower and jumped back into transcribing her notes for the session. She had to finish this tonight.

NOTES:

Career planning is a lifelong process of assessing our strengths, selecting an occupation, locating career opportunities, developing oneself in a career, and then repeating the process as necessary. This cycle may happen once or twice in a lifetime, but it is more likely to happen several times as our life evolves.

Think of your career as your family's intellectual property. It is an essential resource that you should protect, build, and leverage to earn higher levels of income.

Nothing in life is certain, and it is said that "life is what happens when we are busy making other plans." Nonetheless, we can minimize the impact of inevitable twists and turns by having a solid career plan that serves as a guideline for our aspirations. The process of building a plan helps us gain clarity about our goals and identify the resources required and serves as an outline for decision-making in uncertain times. Members of underrepresented groups can benefit significantly from this process, to balance the inherent risks in organizations that are still learning how to fully leverage inclusion.

Here are several questions to help you gain clarity and focus your efforts toward your career goals. [Have participants fill in answers and then reconnect with their partner within twenty-one days to review answers.]

UNDERSTANDING YOURSELF

- What is the worst job you have ever had?
- What parts of it did you dislike the most?
- What is the best job or role you have ever had?
- What parts of it did you like the best?
- How would you describe your current job?
- What parts of your current job do you like the most?
- What parts of it do you dislike the most?
- How long have you been in this role?
- When would you like to transition out?

UNDERSTANDING YOUR STRENGTHS AND WEAKNESSES

- What are you better at than most people?
- What would you do all day for free?
- What are your strengths?
- What are your weaknesses?
- Is there an assessment available to help you identify your strengths and weaknesses?
- What kinds of tasks drain your energy?

IDENTIFYING YOUR CAREER ASPIRATIONS

- What are your career goals?
- Have you done any assessments to confirm that they are a realistic match and personal fit for you?
- Do you need to adjust? Is there someone who can give you objective advice?
- What is your second-round career goal? (Could be the same as original answer.)
- Why does this job appeal to you?

- What is the greater good that will come of you being in this role?
- What would you need to be qualified for this job?
  - education
  - work experience
  - formal training
  - informal mentorship
- What jobs would prepare you for this role?
- What kind of volunteering experience would help prepare you for this role?
- Where can you move laterally?
- What position(s) would you have to be promoted into?
- What have you already accomplished to prepare for this role?
- What do you still need to do to prepare for your next role?

ACTION ITEMS

- What do you need to do next?

RESOURCES REQUIRED

- What resources do you need?

PEOPLE CONNECTIONS

- Who do you need to connect with?

DEADLINE

- When do you need to complete this action?

ROLE №1
ROLE №2
ROLE №3

INTERNAL CAREER PLANNING

- Moving around inside a company can be an excellent way to develop your skills and gain experience that you may not have externally.
- Is your next role inside your existing company?

HAVE YOU:

- Had a career discussion with your current leader? With your mentor? Advocate? Sponsor?
- Shared your career goals?
- Received feedback on strengths and areas for development?
- Requested support for development opportunities (formal or informal)?
- Volunteered for special projects?
- Clarified expectations to be considered "high-potential"?
- Discussed potential roles for the future and time frames?

IMPORTANT QUESTIONS TO ASK YOURSELF

- What kind of career development adds the most value for your job? In your industry (on-the-job experience, special assignments, formal training)? What kind of career development is the most recognizable? Credible?
- Who offers that development?
- When is it offered?
- How much does it cost?
- What is the process to have professional development approved and paid for by your company?
- If it isn't covered by your employer, are you willing to invest in yourself?
- What might you have to give up to make that investment?

- Do you have any blind spots about your performance or personality?
- Is there an established assessment used in your company to identify talent? Have you taken it?
- Do you need additional job skills, experience, or information?
- What areas of yourself will you need to develop?
- Do you need to develop a wider network or links with specific people?
- Do you need to find ways to demonstrate your skills and knowledge so you can provide evidence of what you can do?
- Who can you ask for objective feedback on …
  - Your work product?
  - Your professional skills?
  - Your overall effectiveness at work?
  - Your career opportunities?
  - Your interpersonal skills?
  - Your personal effectiveness in social settings?
- Who might be willing to mentor you:
  - Formally?
  - Informally?
- Who knows about your current work and future potential?
- Do you have a diverse list of people above? (racial mix, tenure and experience, internal/external to your company, etc.)
- Do they know about your goals?
- Have you asked them for their support to help you reach your goals?
- Are they willing to lend their credibility on your behalf as an advocate when you aren't around?

- Do you have a mentor with whom you can discuss both the technical content and the intangibles of your job?
- Who do you admire that you could use as a virtual mentor? (Observe them and learn from their life from afar.)
- Do you feel in charge of your own career direction? If not, how can you gain more confidence and take charge?

CREATING A PERSONAL BRAND

Just like products have an identity, you, too, should have a distinct way of differentiating yourself from other employees.

- What are you best known for at work?
- How would others describe you?
- Does it match how you would describe yourself? How you want people to describe you?
- What experience do you want people to have of you when they first meet you? Or interact with you over time?
- How would you characterize the brand you want to be known for? What would be your tagline?
- What would you need to do consistently to create that experience?
- How should you describe your role in the company to support your brand? (Twenty-five words or less)
- What sound bites should people hear from you and others to support this message?
- Do you need to reassess your appearance, speech, mannerisms, or anything else to be congruent with this brand?
- Are there any changes you could make to the way you deal with people or work situations that might increase your likelihood of achieving your goals? How will you start to do this?

CREATING PLAN B

- What is your plan B in the event you (or your employer) decide that you need to leave within two weeks?
- What short-term job opportunities are available to you? (Within two to six weeks)
- What skills do you need to keep fresh? What certifications to you need to maintain?
- Who do you need to stay in touch with?
- What resources are available to you for job searches?
- Do you know of industry recruiters?
- What could you do to earn money quickly?
  - $500?
  - $5,000?
  - $10,000?

ACTION ITEMS

- Recommend Ginny Clarke's book—*Career Mapping: Charting Your Course in the New World of Work*
- Create a recording of you describing your ideal day. Add multisensory details about what you see, hear, touch, smell, and feel around you. Listen to it often to remind yourself of your ultimate career goal.

"I'm off to a good start." Roshunda caught herself talking out loud. She looked at her watch and realized it was 2:00 a.m. She had been so engrossed in her work, it hadn't seemed to matter.

10

CHANGING
ORGANIZATIONAL CULTURE

Susan was sad to lose LaToya. She was so much more than a "regrettable loss" on a scorecard. In her last few weeks with the company, LaToya had provided what felt like thousands of dollars of free consulting that Susan wished she'd had years ago. Those conversations helped Susan to realize how much is really lost when any employee is not given the opportunity to leverage their strengths and contribute their best to a company. Between LaToya's departure and her coaching from Jim, she felt better equipped to take on the issue of understanding her company's culture and leveraging 100 percent of their diverse talent.

She made one additional strategic move to secure funding to hire Jasmine to help her craft and execute their new culture shift initiative. After many conversations, focus groups, and interviews, Susan was looking forward to having Jasmine present to the senior leadership team today. Jim had spoken so highly of her and the work she and her team were doing with his company. His senior leadership team had seemed to hit a point where they really "got it" about ninety days after they initially received the results of the talent audit. There had been a few bumps and bruises along the way, but Jim seemed very pleased with the formal and informal indicators that things were being done differently.

Susan understood the differences in their approaches. Jim was using his authority to directly address the talent issues for people of color. She was attempting to create a game plan to change her company's culture to be more agile, cutting edge, and modern. She made the business case that their overreliance on the nostalgia that supported their success thus far was beginning to be a burden that cost them clients, innovation, and revenue. She could see where this old-school approach often encouraged unconscious bias, so she'd asked Jasmine to address that directly.

Jasmine launched the meeting, built rapport with the group, and asked them a few introductory questions before she started. "Many companies are beginning to understand the critical role that organizational culture plays in their business success. Much of what we have been trying to solve as diversity and inclusion or inspiring innovation is, at its core, a culture issue. Changing behavior requires focused attention on culture. Getting large numbers of people to do things differently requires a targeted intervention in service of long-term business goals and short-term employee buy-in. Shifting an entrenched culture is one of the toughest tasks that senior executives face, and it requires a higher-than-average degree of leadership fortitude and strategic intervention. Congratulations on joining the movement." She paused and waited for confirmation that everyone was on the same page.

"Our firm has developed what we call a 'daring approach' to organizational change," she said as she showed them the following list:

- Decide that you are serious about this transformation, and then do it.

- Allocate the resources (time and money), and hold people accountable for the process and the results.

- Review and revamp existing policies, procedures, systems, and people who are operating contrary to the future you want to start.

- Execute the changes required, and evaluate the results on an ongoing basis.

After she gave them a chance to ingest the information, she continued, "There are usually at least four hurdles to changing an established organizational culture. The first is cognitive—people must have some understanding of why the change in culture is needed. The second is limited resources—inevitably, changing an organization will require shifting resources away from something toward something else. The third hurdle is motivation—ultimately, individuals have to want to make the change. And the final hurdle is institutional inertia—established ways of working have a very strong energy of their own. We offer four steps to overcoming these hurdles." Again, Jasmine referred to the list and allowed the employees to take in the information.

1. Create an experience of why the change is necessary. Look for ways to demonstrate the harsh realities that make it necessary.

   □ Example: Get clear about the burning platform for the change, and create a campaign to share the story (not necessarily facts and figures) consistently over time. Include a short list of key changes that must occur and link it to a future state that people can embrace.

2. Recognize that you won't be able to convert everyone, nor will it happen overnight. Start with people who have a disproportionately large amount of influence in the orga-

nization. Get them committed to the change, and shine a spotlight on their accomplishments so that others get the message. If they choose not to change, get them out.

- □ Example: Once the communication engine has started, penalize people who rebelliously engage in old behaviors. Select, train, and engage ambassadors who will spread the message and model the new behaviors.

3. Redistribute resources toward activities that require relatively few resources but result in large change—and away from areas with large resource demands but relatively low impact.

- □ Example: Spend money on initial orientations, formal trainings, and informal communications that reach large numbers of people in a short period of time. Speed is essential to counteract institutional inertia. Stop funding visible projects and events that represent the old way of operating.

4. Appoint a senior-level change champion and make them financially accountable for the effectiveness of the change. Recruit additional change champions in strategic roles and departments, in all aspects of the business, and incent them toward the success of the change. Build coalitions at lower levels in the organization who will be the "boots on the ground" troops to execute the everyday tasks, to create and sustain progress. Get rid of people with significant influence who hinder the change.

"Let me stop here and see if there any initial questions." Everyone seemed mesmerized by hearing such an impactful plan outlined so succinctly. They seemed to enjoy Jasmine's no-nonsense approach and were attentive as she continued.

"When organizations decide to change the culture around diversity and inclusion, they often struggle with how to make this change and sustain the progress over the long term. After twenty-plus years working with Fortune 500 companies, the government, and nonprofits, I have concluded that unconscious bias awareness, emotional intelligence training, and good old-fashioned accountability are the three most effective focus areas to effect change in this area.

"So what exactly does all this mean?" she asked. Then she looked around the room and continued. "Unconscious bias refers to a bias that we are unaware of, and which happens outside of our control. It is a bias that happens automatically and is triggered by our brain making quick judgments and assessments of people and situations influenced by our background, culture environments, and personal experiences. Your background, personal experiences, societal standards, and cultural context can have an impact on your decisions and actions without you realizing. For example, a recruiting department may have an established list of "preferred" schools that they recruit from that mirrors the alma maters of hiring managers and/or senior leaders."

Jasmine pointed to the glowing PowerPoint behind her.

"It is a business threat that can result in the following."

- Impacts your retention rate of diverse talent

- Reduces your ability to attract top talent

- Puts your brand and public image at risk, in extreme cases

- Reduces output when it creeps in

- Has significant opportunity costs to engagement and innovation

"So how does it show up in companies?" Jasmine asked, then continued. "Companies develop accepted ways of working that fail to challenge or accommodate individual biases. "That's just the way we do it" becomes the justification that perpetuates behaviors that supports biases. For example, the military established an institutionalized bias against braided hairstyles for women in combat that was only recently challenged. That bias did not take into consideration that the style was very well suited for combat conditions."

Jasmine paused and continued. "What can companies do about it? First, we have to become willing to admit that biases exist as a normal part of brain function. We are not bad people for having them. However, we have a responsibility to identify our individual and organizational biases and actively work to minimize their impact on our decision-making in the workplace. The question is not 'Do we have bias?' but rather 'Which biases do we act on?'

1. *Teach*: Teach your leaders the important elements of unconscious bias.

   a. Teach leaders about the financial impact of unconscious bias and the consequences of conscious bias. Notwithstanding all of the great work that your diversity and inclusion, leadership development, and corporate communications departments are doing, there is a phenomenon that is working against you every moment of every day. It is the unfortunate combination of unconscious bias and the perpetuation of negative stereotypes about people of color.

   People within the organization must become aware of the impact of unconscious bias on their decision-making through various forms of education.

This will help them realize and accept that we all have bias and learn to watch for it in themselves as much as possible. We might think of it as similar to what happens when we step on the clutch in a standard-transmission automobile. The motor doesn't stop running, but it stops moving the car. When we are aware of our biases and watch out for them, they are less likely to blindly dictate our decisions.

b. Teach your leaders emotional intelligence skills. Help them to

» increase their personal and social awareness and
» improve their ability to manage themselves and social situations around them.

2. *Support*: Support your leaders to do the best job possible.

a. Invest in human resources and talent management professionals who can support well-meaning leaders to do a good job. Leadership is a discipline of its own, but somehow it is treated as a "thing" that leaders are supposed to do well in addition to their original subject matter expertise. That may or may not be a realistic expectation, depending on the individual leader, their span of control, or other contributing factors. Having a strong bench of HR support professionals allows for strategic searches in diverse pools, thoughtful planning of fair performance reviews, and qualified coaches on hand to redirect behavior.

b. Resist the urge to cut this budget in the predictable contraction cycle of the fiscal year.

3. *Expect*: Expect behavior and results to change by actively holding people accountable.

    a. Create scorecards with only relevant metrics, and share them broadly and frequently. Decide what results really need changing.

    b. Make sure that senior leaders are asking the right questions to ensure that scorecard activities are happening.

    c. Automate the accountability process with technology where possible. Invest in system-driven reporting that can be delivered on a recurring schedule automatically. Schedule regular meetings to discuss actions being driven from metrics.

4. *Penalize*: Penalize the people who engage in counterproductive behaviors. We have been conditioned to focus on positive outcomes, and we often avoid negative consequences. However, losing someone over what not to do allows others to see what bad looks like and the outcomes associated with failure.

5. *Reward*: Reward the people who are doing it right. Diversify the rewards offered based on what is meaningful to them. In order for money to be an effective reward and an accountability tool, there must be a clear line of sight, span of authority, and ability to influence outcomes where compensation is tied to outcomes. When done properly, this is a very effective element of strategic culture change."

Raymond, the SVP of customer service, spoke up first and posed the question that many others may have been thinking: "Won't all of this seem like white males aren't valued anymore? Like we don't need them?"

Jasmine addressed his question quickly. "I understand how this may seem like that from your perspective, Raymond. On one hand, we are definitely talking about doing things differently than we have before. On the other hand, we are not suggesting mass firings of white males."

Everyone chuckled but needed a follow-up comment from Jasmine quickly. "I understand that you have been trying for some time to shift your culture around inclusiveness. Race in talent management is one of many areas that must be addressed directly—just like we would for any other business challenge. We have to do two difficult things simultaneously:

    a. admit that the results have been skewed in favor of white males to date and

    b. face the reality that this will create discomfort and potentially resistance from the majority of the population.

"As a group, are you all ready for that?" Jasmine looked around the room.

Raymond shrugged his shoulders and gave a melancholic sign of approval. He wasn't convinced just yet but was willing to wait and see.

Rebecca chimed in. "I have a question. Maybe it is more of a confession. I think that white managers are still uncomfortable with this issue of race. I'm not convinced that they—really, *we*—know how to lead through this difficult issue. There is so much behind the dynamic and legal issues—it's hard." As general counsel for the corporation, her insight and honesty was welcomed.

Jasmine responded. "You're right, Rebecca. And you of all people get to see the direct outcomes when conversations go wrong. Vernā Myers and I were emailing about this exact thing the other day. Let me read what she said when I asked her about the business rationale for having conversations about race at the workplace: 'Because employees and customers don't exist in a vacuum, they are affected by the racial and ethnic issues that impact their neighborhoods, families, and the society as a whole. Racial conversations in the workplace can be perceived as dangerous and uncomfortable, but ignoring the impact of racial and ethnic differences on employees and customers can make an organization seem afraid and out of touch and cause it to miss potential problems and opportunities. When race dialogues are planned and well facilitated, they help employees gain a better understanding of each other's perspectives and experiences with racial issues within and outside the workplace. These conversations can break down the barriers posed by implicit bias and stereotypes, lift morale, increase comfort among employees, and enhance team effectiveness. Barriers to the success of employees of color are often uncovered in these settings and, when addressed, can improve their performance, retention, and advancement. Furthermore, being able to talk about race increases employees' comfort and ability to interact with diverse customers and clients in more innovative, sensitive, and respectful ways. And the company's willingness to engage in these conversations demonstrates its commitment to its values of fairness and equality. This demonstration also strengthens the company reputation in the larger community. Ultimately, making space for valuable employees and community members to talk about the important issue of race informs the company of its responsibility as a good corporate citizen, to help eradicate racism and its negative impact on the society in which it operates.'"

After reciting the email, Jasmine asked, "Does that answer your question?"

Everyone nodded, and Rebecca offered a formal response. "It sounds like the benefits outweigh the risks."

"Yes, and it is important to realize that it takes time to create an environment for these conversations to yield the benefits we are talking about. This is not an overnight solution. I don't pretend to have all the answers, but I wrote an article for a trade journal a few months ago titled 'Leading While White.' It offers a few ways for leaders to create that kind of environment. I would be happy to share it with you all, if you think that would be helpful. We can also talk about additional tactics to prepare the organization for these conversations." Everyone nodded as Jasmine wrote herself a reminder note, then transitioned to her final point. "The Mizzou students have taught us all a few key lessons on leadership:

1. People will hold you responsible for what you do and what you don't do.
2. Collaboration and alignment of the allies can become the only data that matters.
3. Leaders serve at the pleasure of the people. To some extent they decide who leads them.

"It won't be long before their approach makes its way out of academia and into corporate America. My recommendation is to be proactive about creating an inclusive culture so that you become better able to react to negative situations."

When it was time to wrap up, Jasmine said, "My role will be to help you think through the key talking points and create a consistent message platform that will be backed up with visible actions. Our next session will focus on identifying key elements of your culture and clarifying your role as senior leaders."

As the employees filed out of the room, they gave Susan initial positive feedback that demonstrated she was on the right track. As she drove home, Susan was pleased with how the meeting had turned out.

She was excited to share her success with Jim and get his insight on what she should expect next. It was such a benefit that his company was so much further ahead of hers on this journey. Before she got out of the car, she took one last look at her email. Jasmine had sent the article she'd mentioned. Even though she was tired and hungry, she couldn't resist the urge to sit in the car and read.

LEADING WHILE WHITE:
TIPS FOR LEADERS WHO WANT TO MOVE THE NEEDLE ON INCLUSION
BY JASMINE MILLS, CPTD

This is a terrible title for this article for three reasons:

1. Effective leadership works for everyone;

2. Nothing that follows will work for every situation;

3. Much of what follows is true for race/gender/generations/ *[insert diversity element here]* in the workplace.
   Nonetheless, this is a good starting place to explore specific approaches to leadership in the context of workplaces where African Americans are typically the minority and where there are barriers to them moving up in the organization.

1. Assume that everything else you have ever learned about leadership is true and applicable when race is a factor. After twenty-two years of working in human resources and talent management in America, twenty-five years total working internationally, and having an MBA in leadership, I am convinced that the secret to effective leadership is becoming someone that other people want to follow.

2. In the absence of unlimited time and budget dollars, I would focus on three concepts to become that person.

- Emotional intelligence: improve your understanding and interactions with yourself and others.

- Situational leadership: learn to read situations and adjust your approach accordingly, especially beyond your own preferences.

- Managerial courage: develop the inner fortitude and personal integrity to do what is right for the highest good.

3. Approach leadership as if everyone is different, they know that they are different, and they want you to appreciate their difference. Age-old adages don't work in the new world.

- "I don't see color": you should, because the reality and impact of color differences is being experienced by people of color.

- "I treat everyone the same": you shouldn't, because you are expected to have range in your solutions while simultaneously complying with key elements that must be the same for everyone.

- "I treat people the way I want to be treated": that doesn't work in leadership. The new standard is to treat people the way they want to be treated.

- Resource: Watch Ted Talk: "Color Blind or Color Brave?" by Mellody Hobson

4. Understand the phenomenon of unconscious bias and accept that

   - everyone has inherent biases that exist just below the surface;

   - they are perpetuated by society; and

   - the best we can hope for is to become a student of our own biases and increase our ability to stop ourselves when they are operating.

5. What works is to look for ways that your bias may show up consciously and unconsciously. What surprises you? What experiences do you prefer? If you made a list of the people you regularly have lunch with, how diverse is the list? How can you diversify that circle?

   - Resource: Watch Ted Talk: "How to Overcome Our Biases" by Vernā Myers

6. Research and understand white privilege, and resist the overwhelming urge to deny it.

   - You didn't create it. It isn't your fault. But it exists. Think of it like the scientific explanation for global warming—just because you don't understand it doesn't mean it isn't influencing your life.

   - Consider that, as a benefactor of white privilege, you have a moral obligation to move through the stages of denial to awareness.

   - It is your human choice to move past awareness to action. Awareness has a powerful energy of its own that may move you to use your privilege in the service of others.

- Resource: "On a Plate," a short story about privilege by Toby Morris http://www. vagabomb.com/This-Comic-Will-Forever-Change-the-Way-You-Look-at-Privilege/

7. Be willing to demonstrate your humanity openly. At the end of the day, people really are the same. It is the context we live in that creates differences among us. As a leader, your primary job is to minimize the experience of context for the people in your organization. Here are a few potential places to start:

  - Start with common ground. Find out what you have in common with people who appear different from you. Engage in meaningful conversations. Be vulnerable enough to let them see the things you struggle with. Share elements of your diversity that may not be obvious to others. Establish connections that you can build on.

  - Build trust by sharing your mistakes and how you learned from them. Remember that the dynamic of corporate America may not always allow others to recover from mistakes as easily as you have. Look for ways to move others forward and allow them the benefit of being, learning, and growing as well.

  - Enlist professional help to have facilitated conversations from experts who specialize in this area. Expect some discomfort, but trust that it will grow into confidence with practice. Look for ways that this experience in the workplace supports your growth in other areas of your life.

- Resource: Look in the mirror and ask yourself, What parts of my career journey can I take 100 percent credit for? Are there any outcomes that feel like success in spite of you? Do you feel any responsibility for using your influence in service of others? Beyond your own success, what kind of impact do you want to have on your workplace? What actions can you take to make that happen?

As she finished the article, Susan decided to forward it to the senior leadership team as originally planned and added an agenda item to assign it as a preread and discussion topic for her next HR team meeting.

11

WORKING WHILE WHITE / WORKING WHILE BLACK

Roshunda's training session with the business resource groups was a big hit, and she received a follow-up assignment. During the career conversation, an employee used the phrase "working while white." The group thought that it would be great to hold a series of lunch-and-learn sessions to explore these concepts a little further, learn more about each other's experience, and cross-pollinate what they wanted each other to know.

As her brain replayed the depth of the conversation, Roshunda wondered if she was in over her head. These were serious topics designed to help each of the groups understand each other better. She knew that employees were passionate about having these conversations, and they were very respectful of each other. She wasn't worried about them—but she second-guessed her facilitation skills and wondered if she could do this topic justice. All of a sudden, she found herself longing for Maya's wise counsel and sound advice. So she picked up the phone and called her.

"Hey, girl. How are you?" Maya sounded so happy to hear her friend's voice.

"Oh my God. I miss you so much," Roshunda confessed.

"Me too. I miss you guys so much. Life is good. Kids are good. Sun, sand, and beach every day. But there's nothing like having my peeps nearby. What's up?"

"Where do I start?" Roshunda's voice changed as she faced the real reason for the call.

"Okay, wait, let me pour more wine. All right, now I'm ready. What's going on?" Maya sounded like she was settling in for the extended debrief.

"I love the new job in HR. I'm learning … I'm growing … I'm scared to death!" Roshunda almost yelled.

"Good. Good. That's a great start. Tell me more," Maya responded in her normal matronly voice that made Roshunda feel better already.

"I facilitated my first employee session on career planning, and I guess it went okay because now they want me to lead a series of lunch and learns. And I—"

Maya stopped her midsentence. "Okay. Stop right there. You need to rephrase that." Maya seemed to scold her.

"What do you mean?" Roshunda asked.

"You were about to miss an opportunity to tactfully promote your success. But you glossed right over it. Obviously you did an awesome job because another assignment came out of it. But you were too busy being humble and minimizing your accomplishment. That's part of why others get ahead of us. We haven't mastered the art of appropriate self-promotion. Start over and try that again."

Roshunda got it. "The employee development session I facilitated on career planning was very well received. The participant feedback indicated that the content hit the mark. The discussion was so rich that the employees asked me to facilitate a follow-up series called 'Working while White, Tips for Understanding Each Other Better.'"

"Bravo! That was awesome! Didn't that feel good? It's all in the messaging. So now what are you scared of?" Maya's feedback was exactly what Roshunda had needed.

"These sessions are going to get into the nitty-gritty of working while Black and working while white. Who knows what kind of topics they will come up with? I don't know if I'm ready for that kind of conversation."

Maya took a deep breath and said, "First, you have to believe in your own ability. Your education, experience, and expertise have all prepared you for a time such as this. You have to drink your own Kool-Aid before you can serve it to others. Stop second-guessing yourself. Your confidence shouldn't be based on what you see around you. Your confidence should be based on what you know inside of you." Maya paused long enough for that last point to land in Roshunda's subconscious and take up permanent residence. Then she continued.

"Once you slay that first dragon of self-doubt, I would hold leader and employee sessions separately: some topics don't work as well in mixed company. Set the room up with round tables; that promotes open dialogue. Establish ground rules for confidentiality, respectful listening, and an agreement to assume positive intent from each other. Establish your role as someone to ask questions; you are not there to provide answers. In fact, there are no right answers, just a series of opinions we agree to respect."

"Okay." Roshunda agreed to all of Maya's suggestions.

Maya continued. "And no recording of any kind, except a few posed shots you put in the company newsletter."

They both laughed and had an unspoken understanding that these conversations represented uncharted waters for the company and Roshunda. However, there was no reason to expect anything other than productive conversation among adults who ultimately had the same goal to better understand each other and have a more cohesive workplace.

While Roshunda was on the phone with Maya, she noticed the email she was waiting for had arrived.

From: Jenny Keller

To: Roshunda Rivers

Subject: Tips for Working while …

Hi Roshunda:

Thanks so much for the awesome career planning session! Your experiences were such an inspiration for those of us who think about doing something different but want to stay with the company.

It was such a rich discussion of how different races experience the workplace. I love the idea of having follow-up lunch-and-learn sessions. As you requested, we had a couple of brainstorming meetings to create the discussion points.

Here are our thoughts on:

- Working while White: attached here

- Working while Black: attached here

Future sessions will include:

- Working while Hispanic

- Working while Asian

- Working while Female

- Working while Gay

We look forward to having you facilitate these sessions and continue the conversations.

Call me if you have any questions,

Jenny

Roshunda opened the attachment and read.

TIPS FOR WORKING WHILE WHITE

- Assume that you are understood. Assume that your colleagues do not hold you personally responsible for society's
issues with race. Assume that your coworkers know that you
are a good person and that you care about all people. Let go
of any feelings of guilt over what has happened in the past.
Start each day with a clean slate, assuming that you will be
judged only by that day's interactions and how you show up
to the people you work with.

- Seek first to understand: Take a moment to breathe and be
present to the reality of why race continues to be an issue in
America. As uncomfortable as it is, can you intuitively feel
what the experience looks and feels like to nonwhite people?
Consider for a moment that Eric Gardner died pleading to
have the breath you just took. Learn what the key issues are.
Sit and watch the footage that launched #ericgardner, #walter-
scott, #sandrabland, #samdubose. Realize that the cumulative
effect of multiple name-specific hashtags in rapid succession
created the need for #blacklivesmatter. This movement did not
spring up randomly. If there was evidence that it was true—
there would be no need for a hashtag.

- Assume that Black people would prefer not to have this
struggle. Assume that they would prefer not to have to worry
about their safety, that they would prefer to have a truly level
playing field in the workplace, and that they would prefer not
to have to talk about race in the workplace either. Assume

that this entire situation is as awkward for them as it is for you. Assume that *awkward* is not nearly the word for the magnitude of this experience for them.

- Help your colleagues to trust that you truly "do not have a racist bone in your body" by demonstrating your compassion and humanity by breaking the silence. Notice when your expression of compassion is necessary and when your silence will scream that you agree with the injustice. Do not use #alllivesmatter. It is the emotional equivalent of going to a breast cancer walk and screaming, "All diseases matter." Not understanding this fundamental point makes it difficult for others to believe your claim of not being biased.

- Consider that if the police brutality occurring in the US was happening anywhere else in the world, we would call it terrorism and a violation of human rights.

- Think of the attacks in Paris as the equivalent effect of what police brutality feels like to Black Americans every day.

- Notice inequality in arenas outside of work. For example, the difference in media coverage and world response to the terrorist attacks in France and Kenya. Almost the same number of people killed but a magnified outpouring of empathy and public support for France. Examples: amount of airtime dedicated for coverage, world leaders offering support, creation of the French flag as a Facebook overlay.

- Build relationships with colleagues who are different from you by engaging in conversation and asking questions about what you don't understand. If you are concerned about offending someone at work, practice with someone outside of your workplace. Seek advice from another person of color in your social circle, and practice having conversations that build trust.

- Understand their use of the N-word and realize that it isn't as mysterious as you may think. Simply put, context matters. Like it or not, African Americans can use this term among themselves, but you cannot. Ever.

  There are two things to understand. First, why are you uncomfortable hearing it? Use of the N-word began as a derogatory term for slaves used exclusively by white people. When you hear it, you are reminded of a painful past that you would prefer to forget (and have others forget, too, if possible).

  Secondly, you should understand how and why it is used so freely now among African Americans of younger generations. Older African Americans tend not to use the term. At some point, the younger generation shifted the negative connotation of this word to become a form of address and even a term of endearment between themselves. It was never intended to give anyone else license to use the word. This process of psychological manipulation changed the meaning and energy of this piece of language based on their membership in the group.

  Similarly an African American man can call his buddy "my boy" or "that boy" and the underlying connotation is admiration and respect. A white man or woman should not use that term because, historically, grown men were referred to as "boys" as a deliberate sign of disrespect. Context matters.

  Another example: an older white lady or any female can refer to other women as girls. Men should never refer to women as girls. The context of this difference is the issue of gender equality and the struggle for women to vote, be treated fairly, and compensated equally (still working on that last one).

A woman without her man is nothing.

A woman: without her, man is nothing.

There are probably tons of other examples to make this point. However, in the case of the N-word, the opposing emotional histories cloud our ability to understand what is simply the fact that context matters. Respecting each other requires us to also respect each other's experience with language.

- Read articles like "Why Is It So Hard to Talk to White People about Racism?" by Dr. Robin DiAngelo. Accept that the very nature of white privilege makes it hard to recognize that it exists. But, just like gravity, not being able to explain it doesn't mean that it isn't affecting you.

- Trust that conversation matters and that dialogue really is a powerful force for change.

WORKING WHILE BLACK: TIPS FOR BLACK / AFRICAN AMERICAN PEOPLE

- Seek first to understand the reasons why race is such a difficult topic for people to engage around.

- Help your colleagues to overcome their unconscious incompetence—fancy words for the fact that sometimes "they don't know what they don't know." For example, calling an African American colleague "articulate and well spoken" may be intended as a compliment, and the speaker may have no idea why it can be considered offensive.

- Be sensitive to the challenges of other groups. Several years ago, I had a white male who reported to me. He came back from a meeting and was visibly upset. He finally admitted to being infuriated by a comment made by a very senior male executive who said, "Guess you still aren't ready to be promoted." This was a direct reference to his facial hair. The executive was retired from the military and held the belief that clean shaven was the standard for male leaders. The feelings of isolation I previously had about my braids morphed into empathy for his facial-hair issue. I realized that many of us make choices that might be burdensome. Other groups, for example, the LGBT community, differently abled individuals, and other ethnic groups, have workplace challenges as well.

- Learn to discern what to ignore. In some cases, you may have an "SMH" response to the example above. Use your judgment to operate somewhere between dangerously dismissive and appropriately direct. Letting everything slide doesn't benefit the rest of us. At the same time, not everything is worth following up on.

- Accept that the history of these interactions have left scars on both sides. Your experiences have created biases that could cause you to make incorrect assumptions.

  After doing all of the above, if the situation calls for a teachable moment, provide one. In the event of a comment or action that offends you or a member of another group, here are a few potential approaches:

- Send a clear message that the comment or action did not land as intended. At some point ignoring offensive comments is no longer an option. Be courageous enough to be the lone voice of dissent in an awkward situation. Leverage your authority and influence when necessary. Spend career equity if the situation screams for someone to speak up. Rather than being afraid of negative repercussions, you might be surprised by the respect others gain for you.

- Be open to the situations when you are in fact the problem. Be objective, open minded, and self aware enough to notice when your behavior is the real issue. If you are fortunate enough to receive feedback, learn to recognize a long-overdue aha moment and refrain from jumping to the conclusion that you are being discriminated against.

- In some cases, the awareness and understanding that our workplace is not our home could allow you to move past the immediate discomfort. And although you might want to help your organization to move to a place where your choice of hairstyle or facial hair isn't a career-limiting decision, decide when it makes sense to engage in this initiative. Let yourself off the hook for not being a successful change agent in a culture you did not create.

- If you find yourself unable to cope with an environment that continuously makes you feel disrespected or devalued, the onus is on you to find a new workplace or, better yet, start your own business and create the environment you want to work in.

12

FULL CIRCLE

B efore Eli could make arrangements to head to LA, Shane and LaToya announced that they were going to be back in the DC/ MD/VA area for MLK weekend. As soon as Roshunda heard, she told Maya and got her to agree to come back that weekend also. The next thing they knew, it was a full-blown reunion weekend.

Eli and Nathan's relationship was struggling under the weight of the disclosure question. The urge to finally be honest about who he was had become stronger than the desire to keep it a secret. He was ready to tell the world, and Nathan simply was not. He decided that today was the day he would overcome this internal struggle.

"I'm gay," Eli blurted out just as everyone finished the extended greetings, hugs and "I missed yous." Before they got settled in their seats, he said it. Each of them looked at each other as if to confirm that they had heard correctly.

Shane was the first to verbalize his thoughts. "Man, is that what has had you so distant?"

"I guess so. I just had to get that out. I have been trying to say it for a while. I just wanted you guys to know." Eli looked like he was about to burst into tears. Shane stood up, walked around the table, and gave him a huge hug. As the two men towered over them, embracing, the women seemed to search their intellect for words.

"I don't know what to say," Maya confessed. "Maybe all that I need to say is that we love you the same as we always have. Or maybe even a little more when I think of how much courage it takes to share this with your loved ones. We love you, Eli. My hope is that you knew that before and you know it now." She got up and gave him a hug.

Roshunda and LaToya chose not to say anything. They simply walked over and gave Eli a group hug. It seemed odd to see them both so in sync on anything. But the moment spoke for itself.

"This is one of the hardest things I have ever done, personally or professionally. I remember some of our previous conversations before you all knew I was gay. So I know how you feel about same-sex attraction. Maya, I know that you don't understand it. And Shane, I know that this isn't your version of manhood. But I hope that your love is stronger than your need for understanding. And that you have room for other versions of manhood. It makes the world of difference for me to feel your love without judgment. Thank you." Eli sat back as if the weight of the world had just been lifted off his shoulders.

The next day, Roshunda was excited to be representing her company at the Leaders and Innovators awards dinner. She loved award ceremonies on any given day, but knowing that her company was being honored for its work as an industry innovator was even more exciting. She was happy that Maya had agreed to accompany her. It felt good to show off her company's success and share this accomplishment with the closest person to a mother she'd ever had.

When Eli told Nathan about the unconditional outpouring of love he received from coming out to his friends, Nathan had an incredible change of heart. He asked Eli to attend the Leaders and

Innovators dinner with him under one condition. He wasn't ready to have a partner at a professional event, but he was okay with a college buddy visiting from out of town. Baby steps were better than no steps.

It was ironic that LaToya and Shane were attending the dinner also. Shane was in town for the conference, and the EVP of his division asked him and LaToya to be his guests at his table. LaToya wore an incredible purple gown, and they looked stunning together as usual.

They all gasped in disbelief at the irony of how the weekend seemed to come full circle. After exchanging hugs and kisses, they moved quickly to their assigned tables before the program began.

As Jim approached the podium, Susan sat at the head table beaming from the inside out. She was so proud of him, not only because she was married to the night's honoree but for his commitment to what he believed in. He was one of the best leaders she ever had the pleasure of learning from, and he was also a committed family man. He rarely missed any of the childrens' events and made their family a priority in all major decisions.

"Ladies and gentlemen, members of the board, and my fellow honorees. What a humbling experience it is to be recognized among such accomplished professionals. There is nowhere to start but with a sincere thank-you." Jim paused to have a private moment with the 1,500 people gathered to celebrate him and his company's success.

"This will sound cliché, but it is an important truth. I did not expect to win this award. Our company was not even focused on innovation. In fact, the award that I would have predicted would have been one for diversity, equity, and inclusion. That has been my focus for the past twenty-four months. We have reassessed how we work together, we have identified and removed talent management barriers, and we have been deliberate about recreating a culture of collaboration. I thought I was doing diversity work. Who knew that it would ultimately pay off as this prestigious award for innovation?" The audience launched a strong round of applause.

"Before you get too impressed about that initiative, I have a confession. I was not initially focused on diversity and inclusion. In fact, I was sitting comfortably in my own world at a restaurant one evening when I overheard a group of African Americans talking about their experience in the workplace. I wasn't being nosy or creepy. I was just in the right place at the right time to benefit from a conversation that changed my perspective. I learned so much from that conversation that I created an environment for my employees to have more of them. I realized that society creates a context around us that can cloud our decision-making. That context alters what we think about ourselves and what we are certain we know about others. When I became willing to be wrong about everything, I started to do more things right. From the stories I hear around the company now, including the product development experiment that got us nominated, I am convinced that this new culture of authentic dialogue led to the collaboration behind this award. My conclusion is that *conversation matters*. Thank you very much."

The crowd rose to its feet and gave Jim a thunderous standing ovation. From their seats scattered around the room, they all wondered if anyone ever overheard the conversations they'd had. LaToya was curious: if someone had listened in, what would they have done with what they'd heard?

AFTERWORD

WHAT NOW?
BY HOWARD J. ROSS

We live in challenging times, especially regarding our conversations about race. Over the past several years, we have seemingly seen an explosion of race-related incidents in the media: the killings of Trayvon Martin, Michael Brown, Eric Garner, and Tamir Rice, and the Charleston church murders; the suspicious deaths of Freddie Gray and Sandra Bland, et cetera. Of course, most of these trends are no different than they have ever been, but the advent of social media and extreme politics has taken them from the back burner to the foreground of our national consciousness once again.

And none of this even begins to address the subtler forms of bias, both conscious and unconscious, that we confront every day and that play out in our workplaces, schools, healthcare institutions, and everywhere else we interact. And yet, despite the constant barrage of these and other incidents in our daily media, at some level we do not have a common consensus among the people in our society that race is still an issue that needs reckoning. For example, a majority of white people believe that whites suffer more discrimination in today's world than African Americans, despite data to the contrary in virtually every aspect of life: jobs, housing, health disparities, incarceration rates, and on and on.

How does this affect us at work? Every day increasingly diverse groups of people show up in their workplaces having read the morning newspaper or watched or listened to their favorite news radio station. We bring our interpretations to work with us and try to form collaborative environments with people of different racial and ethnic backgrounds without talking about race.

It is a hopeless endeavor, because how can we possibly form truly healthy, collaborative environments when we are not even able to discuss the most important issues of our times—issues that impact our relationships every day?

Allison Manswell's *Listen In* is a welcome addition to our discourse around these issues. If you are anything like me, you were probably struck with the authenticity of the characters that Allison introduced us to, and the reality of the conversations that people are either having or trying to find ways to have. Some of the characters might have reminded you of people you know and work with, even people from your own family. You may even have seen some of yourself in one or more of the characters. And yet, we do not always put our thoughts and feelings about race on the table to talk about, particularly in mixed racial groups where the conversations are most needed.

Why are we so frightened about talking about race? There are any number of reasons. We may not want to expose our own pain and frustration. We may be afraid that we will poison our relationships by getting into a controversial and difficult issue to talk about. We may be afraid that we will say the wrong thing and in doing so be branded a "racist" or a "militant" and no longer be seen as just a fellow coworker. We may simply not want to engage in so sensitive or intimate a conversation with the people we work with. At some level, one of the biggest reasons is because we simply have never learned to talk about it. We are afraid of each other and, to some degree, of our own thoughts and feelings and where they might lead us.

And yet, the decision not to talk openly about the topic does not mean that we won't be influenced by it. In fact, we could easily say that our decision not to engage openly with the topic of race almost guarantees that it will have a far greater impact on our unconscious reactions to and relationships with each other. Race is a part of our culture in the United States, and not a part that we are likely to escape from as a core issue any time in our lifetimes. How can we continue to be a great country if we refuse to learn to discuss it?

We also will never be able to achieve what we desire in our organizations unless we are willing to confront the reality of what is. The workforce, workplace, and marketplace are changing faster than any time in our history. Workforces are continually more racially diverse than ever before, as are our marketplaces. The customers we rely on to sustain our businesses are increasingly more diverse and come from different cultural and ethnic backgrounds. The marketplace we work in on a daily basis is increasingly global. We no longer have the choice to "not talk about race" without also refusing to talk about our business. An organization that refuses to create constructive conversations about race will simply not be able to thrive for long in the face of today's demographic landscape.

Allison Manswell has provided a thoughtful contribution to this challenge by giving us a way to conduct these conversations in a meaningful way. She approaches the issue with sensitivity and balance. While providing examples of how people in nondominant racial groups can find ways to deal with the dominant community more effectively, she has not fallen into the trap of encouraging people to *lean in* and act more like the dominant group. While offering ways that members of the dominant group can learn to be more engaged and honest in these conversations, she has not laden people with guilt or judgment. She has, in fact, created an opportunity for authentic human conversation. What a gift!

Listen In does not answer all of our questions. Nor should it. You may not agree with every example, or see yourself having the same conversations that the characters in the book have. So be it. It does not give us a cookie-cutter approach to the right way to do things in every organization, which would be folly. What it does do is make us think about critical issues that impact every American business on a daily basis and give us some thoughtful direction that can help us address what, I believe, is still one of the most critical dynamics of our American conscience. It provides a way that people can come together and work to determine the way their own organizations function. It is a welcome addition to the field.

Thank you, Allison.

Howard Ross is a lifelong social justice advocate and is considered one of the world's seminal thought leaders on identifying and addressing unconscious bias. He is the author of *ReInventing Diversity: Transforming Organizational Community to Strengthen People, Purpose, and Performance* (published by Rowman and Littlefield in conjunction with SHRM in 2011) and the *Washington Post* bestseller *Everyday Bias: Identifying and Navigating Unconscious Judgments in Our Lives* (published by Rowman and Littlefield in 2014). His latest book, *Our Search for Belonging: How Our Need to Connect is Tearing Us Apart*, was released by Berrett-Koehler in May of 2018.

NOTES

INTRODUCTION

1. Sandberg, C., and N. Scovell, 2013. *Lean In: Women, Work, and the Will to Lead.* New York: Alfred A. Knopf, 2013.
2. Brown, Brené. *Rising Strong: The Reckoning. The Rumble. The Revolution.* New York: Spiegel & Grau, 2015.

CHAPTER 1: REFINED BY FIRE

1. Huffington, Ariana. *Thrive: The Third Metric to Redefining Success and Creating a Life of Well-Being, Wisdom, and Wonder.* New York: Harmony Books, 2014.

CHAPTER 4: SILENCE IS A STATEMENT

1. Moore, Wes. *The Work: My Search for a Life That Matters.* New York: Spiegel & Grau, 2015.

CHAPTER 6: JIM MOVES TO ACTION

1. Cooke, Matthew. *Race Baiting 101.* YouTube.com, August 1, 2015. Video file retrieved from https://www.youtube.com/watch?v=lLgIIjnpZyU.
2. Allen, Frederick E. *Howard Schultz to Anti-Gay-Marriage Starbucks Shareholder: 'You Can Sell Your Shares.'* Forbes, March 22, 2013. Retrieved from http://www.forbes.com/sites/frederickallen/2013/03/22/howard-schultz-to-anti-gay-marriage-starbucks-shareholder-you-can-sell-your-shares/.

CHAPTER 8: APPROACHING AWKWARD CONVERSATIONS ABOUT RACE

1. Elliot, Jane. "Jane Elliot." 2015. Retrieved from http://www.janeelliott.com.

CHAPTER 9: PLANNING YOUR CAREER

1. Garrett, E., and G. Clark. *Career Mapping: Charting Your Course in the New World of Work*. New York: Morgan James Publishing, 2011.

CHAPTER 10: CHANGING ORGANIZATIONAL CULTURE

1. Yasmin, Shahana. "This Comic Will Forever Change the Way You Look at Privilege." Vagabomb.com, June 1, 2015. Retrieved from https://www.demilked.com/privilege-explanation-comic-strip-on-a-plate-toby-morris/.
2. Myers, V. "How To Overcome Our Biases? Walk Boldly Toward Them." Ted.com, November 2014. Video file. Retrieved from www.ted.com/talks/verna_myers_how_to_overcome_our_biases_walk_boldly_toward_them.
3. Hobson, M. "Color Blind or Color Brave?" Ted.com, March 2014. Video file. Retrieved from www.ted.com/talks/mellody_hobson_color_blind_or_color_brave.
4. DiAngelo, Robin. "White Fragility: Why It's So Hard to Talk to White People about Racism." The Good Men Project, April 9, 2015. Retrieved from http://goodmenproject.com/featured-content/white-fragility-why-its-so-hard-to-talk-to-white-people-about-racism-twlm/.

ABOUT THE AUTHOR

Allison Manswell is a seasoned talent management executive with over twenty-five years of proven experience in human resources, organizational effectiveness, employee and leadership development, and diversity and inclusion interventions with *Fortune*-ranked companies, mid-size organizations and boutique consulting firms. She is the author of *Listen In: Crucial Conversations on Race in the Workplace* and the sequel, *Someday Is Today: Achieving Racial Equity in the Workplace*.

She holds the industry credential of Certified Professional in Talent Development (CPTD) from the Association for Talent Development. In addition, Ms. Manswell holds an MBA in leadership and has been an on-ground and online faculty member for undergraduate and graduate programs. Her career began with a bachelor's degree in justice and law enforcement and roles with the Royal Canadian Mounted Police and Revenue Canada.

Ms. Manswell is the founder and CEO of Path Forward Consulting, a boutique firm that leverages her expertise in:

- consulting with small, mid-size and large-scale organizations, including assessments and culture shift;
- training from design through delivery and evaluation; and
- coaching from individual contributors to senior executives and groups.

She has grown the firm from a small start-up to a globally recognized industry leader recognized as:

- Top 10 Leadership Development Firm by *HR Tech Outlook Magazine*
- Top 10 Diversity & Inclusion Firm by *HR Tech Outlook Magazine*
- Top 10 Organizational Effectiveness Firm by *Manage HR Magazine*
- Most Influential Race Specialist (USA) by *Acquisitions International Magazine*
- 50 Most Innovative Companies to Watch by *CIO Bulletin*
- 50 Innovators of the Year by *CIO Bulletin*

As a recognized subject matter expert, her media appearances include NBC, NPR, and many contributions to professional conferences. Ms. Manswell is also a sought-after speaker who has worked internationally in the US, Canada, the Caribbean, and Brazil.

Mostly importantly, she is the mother of three sons, who have grown from being her millennial roommates to accomplished young men who are all scholars/athletes/entrepreneurs. Her hobbies include astrology and traveling for family and cultural events where food, music, and dancing are involved.

For more information or to book Allison Manswell,
visit AllisonManswell.com.